POSITIVITY
IS OUR
SUPERPOWER

POSITIVITY
IS OUR
SUPERPOWER

**Everything I've Learned about Trauma,
Grief, Confidence and Self-Love**

MALIN ANDERSSON

HAY HOUSE

Carlsbad, California • New York City
London • Sydney • New Delhi

Published in the United Kingdom by:
Hay House UK Ltd, The Sixth Floor, Watson House,
54 Baker Street, London W1U 7BU
Tel: +44 (0)20 3927 7290; Fax: +44 (0)20 3927 7291
www.hayhouse.co.uk

Published in the United States of America by:
Hay House Inc., PO Box 5100, Carlsbad, CA 92018-5100
Tel: (1) 760 431 7695 or (800) 654 5126
Fax: (1) 760 431 6948 or (800) 650 5115; www.hayhouse.com

Published in Australia by:
Hay House Australia Pty Ltd, 18/36 Ralph St, Alexandria NSW 2015
Tel: (61) 2 9669 4299; Fax: (61) 2 9669 4144; www.hayhouse.com.au

Published in India by:
Hay House Publishers India, Muskaan Complex,
Plot No.3, B-2, Vasant Kunj, New Delhi 110 070
Tel: (91) 11 4176 1620; Fax: (91) 11 4176 1630; www.hayhouse.co.in

A catalogue record for this book is available from the British Library.

Tradepaper ISBN: 978-1-78817-649-1
E-book ISBN: 978-1-78817-653-8
Audiobook ISBN: 978-1-78817-650-7

MIX
Paper from
responsible sources
FSC® C013056

Printed and bound in Great Britain by
TJ Books Limited, Padstow, Cornwall

CONTENTS

INTRODUCTION

I've always wanted to write a book, but the first time I thought about it seriously was after my mum died when I was 25. Little did I know then that the universe still had a bit more to throw at me before I'd get around to working on *this* book about my experiences of trauma and grief.

To be honest, I've endured a lot of traumas in my life, and from the youngest age – my father died when I was 11 months old. Since that challenging start, I've had to overcome childhood bullying, eating disorders, racism, the fickleness of fame, losing my mum to cancer, sexual assault, domestic violence, and the most painful chapter in my life: the death of my child. This book explores the raw wounds that I've been left with, but it's also an acknowledgement of the light that can come after the clouds have passed.

People expect you to be broken after going through so much trauma. And don't get me wrong, I was for a while. But then I guess I found the light. I chose to grow from my experiences. What helped me to find the resilience and strength to heal was discovering my own path and spiritual beliefs and practices. Having my own awakening, if you like.

Actually, I was raised a Christian and my mum was a devout Catholic, so I went to church on Sundays and to Sunday school. But it never made much sense to me – I didn't buy into her Christian beliefs. I remember seeing my mum's body in the morgue and instead of crying as you'd normally do, I just said, 'She looks different.' I had an overwhelming urge to touch her, so I prodded her face. My brother was like, 'What the hell are you doing?' I replied, 'She's gone. I can feel her behind me, but I can't feel her in this body.'

It was after that experience that I started to question *everything*. My mind began to go a bit crazy. I could feel my mum around me. Feathers were constantly in my surroundings – a sign that your angels and loved ones are close and sending you loving reassurance. I think my consciousness just expanded. And from then on, I couldn't go back in time. That was me: I was awake.

For me, writing this book has almost been like therapy. It's been tough because I've had to relive and revisit stuff that was painful, and it brought back a lot of difficult memories. Every one of those traumatic events in my life was a milestone, and in the chapters of this book I openly share my innermost thoughts, feelings and reactions around them.

But I also share the things I've discovered along the way that have helped me, and which might help *you* to feel the sunshine in your life. Because it does come again – it might just take a while. You'll also find some of my favourite mantras, which I use myself, and the tips and tricks that help me to stay in a good place mentally and emotionally. I hope you find all this helpful too.

After I lost my mum and then my baby, Consy, and I'd walked away from an abusive relationship, I remember wandering around my apartment, not really knowing what I was doing. I was a lost girl. I started using my Instagram almost as a blog, just speaking about how I felt after being attacked by my former partner.

The biggest surprise was that other people were comforted by me doing that. And then, as more and more people resonated with my experiences and the messages I shared, I thought: *Well, I've been through other things too, so let me talk about them as well.*

I ended up speaking about everything, whether it was eating disorders, grief or love. And as I was getting more and more responses from people telling me that I was helping them, I thought, *This feels right. This is my purpose. This is definitely my calling.*

Two years later, I now have well over 700,000 Instagram followers, and I'm a motivational speaker and a champion for those with body-image issues or eating disorders. I'm also an ambassador for leading charities that deal with infant mortality, domestic violence, depression, suicide, and other mental health issues. I fight for causes that pain me and which I've had personal and raw experience of.

Despite all this 'success' I'd say that my biggest achievement so far is simply to have gotten through the barriers and to have overcome all the obstacles and traumas in my life. And the thing I'm most proud of is that I'm able to reach thousands of people who perhaps haven't been reached out to before: those who might find themselves thinking that they have no way out and who haven't had the support of someone who's lived the traumas that I've been through.

I want people to realize that they're not victims and that they can survive and come through it, as I did. That's why I've written this book.

So, if you find yourself in a traumatic situation, or you know someone in that dark place right now, this book is for you. What I share in its pages will help you to see that there *is* hope and there *is* another way. After all the heartache I've been through, I'm now thriving, and you can too.

Entering the prospect of motherhood without my own mother was scary and painful. Leaving that road without my mum or my baby was the worst thing I've ever gone through. But I survived, and I want you to know that you will too, whatever it is you're fighting your way through right now.

Chapter 1

TURNING EARLY SETBACKS INTO STRENGTHS

Lessons from My Troubled Start in Life

{ MALIN'S MANTRAS }

Don't be afraid to rock alone.

The Sun is alone every day, and it still shines.

Being alone is when the most growth happens.

It's when you're able to process and heal without anyone else's energy disturbing yours. Use this time wisely.

I've always felt very, very different. But in truth, I've always liked being different. I love being exotic-looking, and even though I'm proud to be English and to have been a finalist in the Miss England beauty pageant, I'm equally proud to say that I'm half Swedish and half Sri Lankan. In fact, I was born in Sweden in a small village called Trollhattan, the youngest of the four children – I have two brothers and a sister – of a Sri Lankan mother and a Swedish father.

I've no recollection of our life in Sweden. My earliest memory is of moving to England when I was three years old. My dad, Rune, had passed away when I was around 11 months old, and even though my mum's sisters lived close by, she wanted to have a fresh start without the constant reminders of life with him. So, we moved to the East of England – to a beautiful little village in Bedfordshire called Houghton Conquest.

As part of a mixed-race, single-parent family, it was quite tough for my brothers and sister turning up in a very white village school, especially as they didn't speak a word of English. Although later we only ever spoke English at home, weirdly, I can still speak fluent Swedish. I guess I just picked it up listening to my mum talking on the phone to her sisters.

An Imaginative Child

Childhood was quite a lonely place for me. Despite having three siblings, I was rather a solitary child and lived in my imagination a lot of the time. I liked to write letters and create short stories. I'd write letters to my mum and put them under her bedroom door. I'd give letters to my teachers and to my brothers and sister, and I also wrote to my dad in heaven.

I still have some of those letters, which my mum collected for me in a book. Writing letters was my way of speaking to people, of expressing myself, and of trying to make sense of the stuff that, as a child, I couldn't process. Looking back, I guess I was journalling, without even knowing what that was. Today, journalling is a tool that's part of my daily practices – I use it to help me make sense of what's happening in my life.

JOURNALLING

As those of you who have followed me for a while know, one thing I do every night before bed (or sometimes in the morning) is journal. I write down what I'm feeling or what I'm thinking, or I jot down the things that are playing on my mind. Or perhaps I'll go for gratitude – so I'll write down some things I'm grateful for.

I think that journalling sets you up for a good, positive and strong day. Jotting down your thoughts in a journal helps you to let go of your worries. When you see things on paper, you're clearing your mind of them – you're literally emptying out your mind. You write it all down, then put away your journal and forget it until you're ready to start again the next day.

I think I was a weird kid. I loved playing outside on the grass and in the mud. I had a wild imagination and liked nothing better than dressing up. I'd pretend to be a superhero or a ninja. I'd hide in a den and pretend that I'd gone missing and that my family had been looking for me for days. I loved playing at all that survival stuff in my den and camping out in the garden.

I had friends in the village who I'd play with sometimes, but I spent a lot of time on my own – I still do. I guess I must have been lonely on occasions though, as I remember knocking on my brother's bedroom door and asking him to play with me. But, typical big brother, he'd tell me to go away.

In truth, losing my dad so young always hung over me, too. I remember being in the playground when I was around four years old and missing him and wishing I had a dad in my life. I can see myself now, walking through the playground on my own and wondering what it would be like to have a dad. How sad is that?

I became massively self-reliant from a young age, too – I had to because I spent so much time on my own and because my mum was ill for much of my childhood. In fact, being alone is a theme that's run throughout my life. For sure, one million per cent, there have been episodes where I've felt so alone and afraid. It's been a big challenge for me to overcome them. But mostly, being in my own company is something I've grown to love and value.

A Mother's Courage

I often think that it must have taken a ton of courage for my mum to move from Sweden to England as a widow with four children in tow. She did have a man in her life here, almost from the outset, and he became a caring father figure to us until she died, but all the same, it was always my mum who was the rock in our family. I drew my strength and inspiration from her example. I'm a lot like her – we shared the same mindset.

My mum was besotted with me, perhaps because I was the youngest and she knew I'd be her last child. I was a proper mummy's girl. Just before she died, she said, 'I know I spoiled you. It was my fault, but I didn't want you to grow up.' Yeah, definitely a mama's girl. I even slept in her bed until I was about nine years old!

One of the things that troubled my mum the most when I was young was that I had no memories of my birth father. So, she'd speak of him often and show me videos of their life together. She told me that as he held me in his arms, he'd look at me and say, 'I'm sorry, Malin,' because he knew that he was dying of cancer.

He had skin cancer three times, but on the third occasion, it spread to his bones. When I was born, he was already terminally ill. He said to my mum, 'Tell Malin that I loved her and that I remember holding her.' Sadly, that's just about all that I really know about him. He was only 49 when he died, leaving my mum a widow at 40.

My dad's death left my mum severely depressed for much of the remainder of her life, which I totally understand. And yet, despite her own problems, she did everything she could for me and my siblings. She worked so hard as a cleaner, saving bits of money where she could, and before she got stomach cancer, she worked for the residential care company Leonard Cheshire for 25 years, looking after disabled people. That's tough work, you know, helping the residents and cleaning up after them. But she did all of that grafting just for us.

She spent a lot of money on me – giving me everything that I wanted – just to make me happy. Same thing with my brothers and sister. In fact, everything she did was for us, which is so, so sweet. Of course, she was trying to compensate for my dad not being in our lives; but in part, it was also because she'd had such a tough upbringing herself and she didn't want that for her own kids.

Humble Beginnings

My mum and her five sisters and brother had been brought up in poverty in Sri Lanka, where they'd lived in a slum. For some reason my mum had been singled out by her parents for regular beatings, and she'd never had enough to eat – this early malnourishment probably contributed to her being barely five feet tall as an adult.

Her parents also constantly told her that she wasn't pretty enough, and as a result, she pushed us all very hard to achieve; it's also why she pushed me into beauty pageants and to become famous.

My mum managed to escape her awful home environment by joining an Irish nunnery. Unbelievably, she was then mistreated by the nuns, who were really cruel. She transferred to a convent in England, but she wasn't happy there either. So, when she saw the lonely hearts advert placed by my dad in a newspaper, Mum jumped at the chance of a way out.

Her older sister happened to be living in Sweden, so Mum responded to the ad in the hope of escaping life in the convent. Thankfully, she ended up falling in love with my dad and found happiness. Up to that point in her life, she'd only ever been treated badly. But importantly, she maintained that it was her tough upbringing that gave her the strength and drive she needed later in life.

It also made her massively protective of her kids. She taught me how to be strong, especially in the face of bullying at school. In her heavy Sri Lankan accent she'd say: 'Walk with your back straight, Malin – you can't let anyone see that you're slouching and weak. If someone says something nasty to you, you look straight back at them like this,' and she'd give me one of her stern, defiant stares.

She was that kind of protective mum. If any of the girls were being bitchy, she'd say, 'You tell them! Do they know who you are? Don't ever let anyone pick on you, Malin.' She was a little pocket rocket – a fierce chihuahua.

⭐ **VIBING HIGH** ⭐

Remember – you're not alone! On the way home from shooting a podcast, I was staring out of the window, looking up into the night sky, when I saw the most beautiful stars. It was almost as if my family were saying 'hang tight'. You're not alone.

Apart from those few years she shared with my dad, I don't know if my mum was ever truly happy. But I know for sure that she was a warrior when it came to her kids. She actually slept with a sledgehammer behind her bed, in case anyone ever broke in.

I remember seeing it and I'm like, 'What the fuck, Mum?' I'll never forget it because she said, 'I'd rather go to jail than let anything happen to you.' And I know that she watches over me and protects me to this day.

Fear of Abandonment

Mum was the anchor in all our young lives, so imagine my terror on the day I overheard a conversation in the kitchen about her having developed breast cancer. I'd already lost my dad, and now my reality, at just nine years of age, was that I might lose my mum, my rock, too. Once my parents realized I'd been eavesdropping, they explained what was happening and tried to reassure me. But it didn't stop the cold fear.

In spring 2002, my mum was taken into hospital to have a lump in her breast removed, and David, my stepdad, visited her every single day. Without fail, I went with him; I never missed a trip to the hospital. I helped to wash my mum, to brush her hair and clean her. I cared for her, even though I was only nine.

And every night, I'd lie under my bedsheets feeling really scared. I'd chant prayers like a mantra: '*Please make sure my mum's okay and she comes back home; please make sure my mum's okay and she comes back home.*' I'd chant them over and over again until I eventually fell asleep.

Following her lumpectomy and the removal of the glands under her arm, my mum was very weak, and she had to stop work. She then had radiotherapy and chemotherapy, and the chemo almost killed her. She was so poorly – she had sepsis, too. For years afterwards she couldn't work much because her hands would swell up and she was generally too weak to do her manual labour job.

Even though at that time I prayed each night for my mum not to die, my worst nightmare did eventually come true in November 2017, when she died of stomach cancer. My biggest fear had come to life, and I'm sure that's why I had such a dramatic shift in mindset after her death.

{ **MALIN'S MANTRAS** }

The good thing about the past is that it's in the past. You no longer have to experience those traumatic events. Stop replaying those memories.

But the truth is that those 15 years between the breast and stomach cancer, when she was clear, gave my mum the time to see me grow up and become a woman – a gift I'll never take for granted.

She witnessed my prime time, my transition into adulthood – starting my periods, having my first boyfriend, my first job as cabin crew. She was so proud of me becoming cabin crew and she loved me turning up in uniform. Thankfully, she saw me blossom, which was amazing considering how ill she'd been.

Looking Within

I'm so grateful for the extra 15 years I had Mum in my life. And yet, during that time, even though she was in remission, the fear of losing her always hung over me. I used to panic sometimes and say to her, 'I don't want you to die.' She'd just laugh and say, 'Don't worry, I'm not going anywhere.'

Despite the ever-present fear of losing my mum, like most teenagers, having fun and going out into the world eventually took over. I became consumed by my social life, work and having a good time, and sadly, I started to take my mum for granted. In fact, in my teens and early twenties, I was a bitch to her, to be honest.

Partly, it was because of the hormonal imbalances and mood swings caused by my eating disorders, but mainly it was because I was an angry, confused young woman. Now, I hate the fact that I was so horrible to her – it's the closest I've come to a regret in my life – but at the time, I wasn't aware enough to know better.

My mum and I had lots of rows when I was a teenager. I'd ask her for money constantly, and I was always asking her to buy this or that for me. I was a real spoiled brat. At first, she'd say no, but then she'd always give in.

What was really bad is that I'd carry on until I got what I wanted. While we were growing up, Mum would pretend to be strict – like, she'd wave a slipper about – but she never hit us. She was a bit of a pushover, really, which is funny considering her own strict upbringing. But she really didn't want that for us. Instead, she showered us with love.

I only overcame my childhood fear of being abandoned when I learned to become whole on my own, without needing anybody else to complete me. And for me, the way to do that was to spend time alone and figure out who I really was.

Slowly, it dawned on me that no one else was making me happy, and that it was only *me* who could make me happy. I used to think that boyfriends could fulfil that role, but they were making it worse. I was seeing friends and trying to fill up my time, but at the end of the day, I was still going to bed alone, and I was there with the thoughts in my head. That's when I realized that nothing external was helping me.

Of course, I read books and they were a useful tool, but ultimately, it was taking a step back and looking at what was going on in my life that helped me the most. Unfortunately, it took a load of crap for me to realize that nothing and no one was going to make me complete. But that was my path.

If you persevere and keep looking within and taking a refresh, you too will come to the realization that nothing outside of you will make you feel complete. It's always going to be just you. And *that's* when you find that you don't need anyone else to add anything to your life and that you no longer need to fear being abandoned.

HEALING THE WOUNDS

For me, time has been the greatest healer. The trauma that we endure at any age, whether it's as a child losing a parent or domestic abuse as an adult, has no quick and easy fix. Each time I say that to others, the clearer the truth of it becomes to me.

We think that we can overcome pain and struggle in an instant, but we can't. We want things now, we want things quickly, but this isn't how life works. If we are to heal, we must allow the process to happen. And by that, I mean taking each day as it comes, allowing yourself to feel how you need to, and focusing on the present moment – not worrying about the future or the past.

I've come a long way from that little girl who lulled herself to sleep with prayers asking God to keep her mum alive. As I reflect on just how far I've come, I tear up because I know my mum would be so proud of me. I didn't stop or give up – I carried on, despite constant pain being thrown at me. And now? Now I continue looking forwards, and not back.

Learning Self-Reliance

Mum's illness and depression while we were growing up meant that we children had to care for ourselves a good deal. I remember having to wash my own clothes when my mum was ill because she didn't think my stepdad, David, was doing it right. Before she went into hospital, Mum showed me what to do.

Even though David was very involved in our lives and did a lot for us – like dropping us off and picking us up from school – I had to do a lot for myself; at the age of nine I was sorting out my clothes and getting myself showered and ready for the day.

These early experiences gave me the strength to be independent, but they also made me quite defensive. To me, it was important to be self-reliant because I knew from bitter experience that ultimately, I couldn't count on the people I loved always being in my life.

To this day, I'm scared of losing people. That's just the legacy of losing both parents at a young age, and of course, losing baby Consy. When someone comes into my life, I'm quite cold-hearted initially. I can easily let them go.

If it's a friend and they've done me wrong, it's one strike and you're out, you know. When I get into a relationship, I'm constantly fearful that the person will either hurt me or leave me – or die. It's quite sad, actually. So, being cautious is my way of protecting myself: my guard is always up.

⭐ **VIBING HIGH** ⭐

My baby, my mum and my papa are now forever protecting me. There's no place for sadness.

As I've explained, it's only now that I realize that the fear of abandonment is an illusion. *We* are all we need. We are one soul and anything else is an add-on to who we are. So, things and people may be taken away from us, but they can never be taken away from our soul because they are just extensions of us, you know. And a fear of abandonment doesn't really exist in my head any more because I know that I'm complete and that everything is here within me.

Of course, this concept is too hard to grasp when you're young. In fact, if anyone had told me this when I was a girl, I wouldn't have wanted to hear it. I'd probably have told them to get lost. Your daddy is all you want when you're little.

Seriously, though, when I was younger, the fear of abandonment was horrible. I think, in my mind, I was wondering, *Will I be an orphan? Where will I live?* And as I got older, I became more aware that losing my mum wouldn't be just losing her as a person but also the way she brought me up: the comfort of her nest and all that she provided. All those things would be taken away, not just the person.

The late American spiritual teacher Ram Dass (I'm a huge fan) said that 'we are all one', and when I look at life like that, despite never really knowing my birth father and losing my mum, I no longer fear people coming in and out of my life. That's just the way the world works. People come in to teach us things and they leave. Then, other people come through and that's all part of the journey.

Malin's Gratitudes

I'm feeling grateful for...

- My family and my upbringing
- My ability to keep giving
- The healing I've received and my health
- My comfort in being alone now
- All the opportunities that life has given me, despite the setbacks and early traumas

Chapter 2

GETTING AROUND
NEGATIVE PEOPLE

Combatting Bullies, Racists and Energy Vampires

{ MALIN'S MANTRAS }

Nobody glows more than a soul who has let the hurt go.

Forgive, and let go of any heavy energy.

Over the years, I've had my fair share of negative people in my life and, I'll be honest, it's taken me a long time to learn how best to deal with them. Sad to say, most of us face bitchiness and nastiness at some stage. For me, it's mainly taken the form of bullying through my school years, racist comments, and professional and personal jealousies as my career has blossomed.

What I've learned is that I don't need negative people in my life. I have a tattoo on my arm that says, 'Observe the time and fly from evil'. Pretty dramatic, right? But now I always follow that advice. I observe and wait for a time, and if I'm not feeling comfortable in a situation, I'll leave.

If something or someone doesn't serve me well, why should I waste my time? I could die tomorrow. I want to spend my time with people where we're adding to each other's lives, not subtracting.

I think I've reached an age where I better understand what life is about. So, if someone's done me dirty or their intention hasn't been pure, I can never look at them in the same way again and I don't want them in my life right now.

I recognize that they're on their journey and that they can change – I'm pretty sure I was there at one point, you know – so I send them love, healing and peace. But at this moment in time, I'd rather not have them around me. I now know that I don't need anyone – or that someone new will come along – and that's how I work. Of course, I didn't know this when I was younger.

Being Bullied at School

In primary school, I was very quiet and shy, and I remember that the bullying started when I got to middle school at the age of nine – around the time that my mum was taken ill. Back then, it's fair to say that I was pretty geeky: in fact, I looked more like a boy. I sat there with my glasses on and my hair all fluffy and sticking out. I also had quite a prominent moustache and sideburns.

The popular, loud kids started calling me Mr Burns, after the character on *The Simpsons*. Sometimes they'd do the Nazi salute at me and call me Hitler because of the facial hair on my upper lip. But mainly, they'd sing 'Ms Dy-Na-Mi-Te-e' at me, because they thought I looked like the British rapper Ms Dynamite, especially after my mum had done my hair and put me in a little pink headband. I also got called a Bounty bar, for being 'brown on the outside and white on the inside'.

My best friend at the time was very badly bullied – they called her Hagrid. I sat next to her in school and together we made an easy target for the taunts. On the bus home, we'd sit at the front while the cool kids sat at the back, but they'd throw food and random objects at us.

I was so shy and awkward at that age, and I just thought, *Is it because I'm ugly? Is it my skin colour? Am I not meant to have sideburns?* I remember getting my sister's razor and trying to shave them off. I never really understood why I was being bullied and I think that led to me having zero self-esteem as a teenager.

The teachers seemed powerless to help. In fact, my PE teacher made it even worse. On one occasion while I was doing gymnastics, she took my hand as I balanced on the beam and went, 'Ugh, your hands are so sweaty!' It gave me a really big complex. She really shouldn't have said that to a little girl – it was cruel.

The bullying really got to me and, when I was 11, I started pulling out my hair. It's a recognized anxiety disorder called Trichotillomania; I'd sit and twist my hair and pull it out in small clumps until I had these little bald patches. My sister, Emma, noticed and she was like, 'What the fuck are you doing?'

'I can't help it,' I told her. 'I just can't help it.' Emma eventually helped me to stop doing it, but when I was on the receiving end of taunts and sneers and I got nervous, I just kept wanting to pull out my hair again.

However, there was one day that I'll never forget. I was looking in the mirror at my fluffy hair and my facial features, and as I turned my face this way and that I wondered how I'd look when I was older. Amazingly, I found myself envisioning how I'd look in 10 years' time, and I said to myself, *I'm going to be really pretty. I'll be like Nicole Scherzinger. I'm going to be really, really pretty when I'm older, so don't worry.*

It was so clear to me – it was a knowing, a certainty, a direct message from the Divine, even. What a cool thing for a kid to do, you know. I always knew I was a weird spiritual being.

{ Malin's Mantras }

This year, make the commitment that no matter how lonely you get on your journey, you will not invite toxic people back into your life. Keep moving forwards, not backwards. Great things are coming if you persevere.

Not surprisingly, I couldn't maintain that sort of self-confidence in the face of the taunts and sneers, and by the time I got to year 8 (age 12–13), I wanted to change my image and to grow up a bit. Emma helped me to straighten my hair and she took me to get my eyebrows threaded. Because of all the bullying I'd endured, I just had this very strong urge to change my appearance. I wanted to be cool and popular.

I was like, *Right, I'm gonna reinvent myself when I get to year 9.* And, just like that, I became popular. Together with my new look, I developed a bit more attitude – you know, answering the teachers back, getting kicked out of science class: I thought that was cool. I got a bit cocky and made jokes.

Then I got myself a cool boyfriend – he was one of the popular boys – and I was in and out of trouble at school for a while. Not in a bad way – I was never extreme with the stuff I did, and I always got away with it – but just enough to appeal to the cool kids. Yet little did I know that the worst bullying of my life was still to come.

HEALING YOUR INNER CHILD

I re-found my inner child after I went through the healing process. Now, in my heart, I'm back to being that weird kid again. I revel in who I am and who she was – I like to play the martial arts fighting game UFC on the PlayStation, or do birdwatching, just as she did.

I believe that our inner child needs to be loved and healed. So, during my hypnotherapy sessions or meditation, I envision my child self and I tell her, 'Everything's going to be all right.' I'm standing next to her, holding her hand and telling her, 'Everything's going to be fine.'

That was quite hard for me to do because I was insecure about how I looked, and I didn't love myself for so long – I never truly healed from that bullying. I remember that little girl, and the way she felt, so clearly. All I cared about at the time was my family, especially my mum, but even so, when other kids are being nasty, some of it sticks with you and it lasts a long time. It contributes to the way you view yourself.

If I hadn't experienced the bullying, I probably wouldn't have wanted to change how I looked so much. I probably would have loved myself more. All of which is so sad. Even now, because of that childhood teasing, I still occasionally feel self-conscious about my sideburns. But in reality, I'm able to embrace my looks and my body entirely. I'm in a great place. And I wanted my inner child to know that this is what she can look forward to.

Ugly Duckling to Swan

When I was 16, my popularity status at school plummeted when some of the cool girls found out that I was entering beauty pageants. There was a lot of verbal abuse: 'Oh, you think you're really pretty, do you?' And online sniping: 'Malin's in Miss Bedfordshire. I don't think so!' When I won some of those contests, it got even worse.

My mum told me it was all just jealousy because I'd blossomed, but whatever the reason, the barbs still hurt. In fact, the bullying and threats became so malicious that I had to spend my lunchtimes in the library with a teacher in attendance.

Suddenly, I'd become an unpopular 'popular' girl, and my only friends were boys. Fortunately, even when I'd been one of the popular girls, I'd never bullied anyone, because I knew what it felt like. So at least the marginalized kids didn't hate me.

When I reached the final of Miss England, the bullying escalated. Some girls wanted to fight me, while others were verbally vicious. My mum would go into the school and demand to see the head teacher. She'd call the school and tell them that this bullying had to stop. But nothing changed. In the end, she was resigned to the school being unable to stop the bullying. 'Just finish your GCSEs, Malin, and be done with it,' she told me. 'You can leave after your exams.'

And I did just that. But it didn't stop Mum dressing me up on mufti days. She made sure I looked proper in nice clothes and makeup, and she'd say, 'Go on, just make them even more jealous.' She couldn't stop the behaviour, so she decided to fight fire with fire.

In the autumn of 2009, I changed schools to do my A-levels, but I didn't want to be there, so I left and went to Bedfordshire's Barnfield College to start a Diploma in Air Cabin Crew. When I was a quarter of the way through the course, I was offered a job with Virgin Airlines, so I left without completing it. I thought, *Thank the fucking Lord. I've been saved.* Then, can you believe it, I got bullied at Virgin!

Bullying at Work

When I look back at that stage of my life, I realize it's no wonder I developed eating disorders and had zero self-esteem. I went from the bullying at school and the pressure to be thin for the pageants, to being weighed in before a flight and inspected to make sure my skirt fitted correctly.

Even my mum, who didn't really understand the pressures, inadvertently contributed. She'd say, 'Come on, Malin, you've gained a little bit of weight. Not too much... well, maybe too much. No, you're looking good. But maybe a little bit of weight gain?' It didn't help.

When I started at Virgin aged 18, I was a quiet, naïve and innocent girl, in a sense. I was very pretty and very skinny, but I was obsessed with my weight and extremely insecure. I was picked on by some of the women in the Virgin cabin staff. They'd say, 'Oh, go and do this', but it would be a fool's errand and I'd get into trouble for it. The all-female crews were extremely bitchy – I just hadn't expected that in an adult environment. I thought I'd left it all behind when I left education.

I had a run-in with one of those experienced female crew members and I was sent home pending an investigation with the manager. In fact, I quit before that meeting because I felt so sick and disgusted that the bullying was still messing up my life. My mum tried to talk me out of it, but my mind was set. I told her, 'I'm not putting up with it any more,' and I left Virgin after only six months.

UNITE AGAINST BULLYING

If you're reading this and the stories of bullying resonate with you, understand that just as it is with trolls, bullies project their own insecurities onto you. You're not what they say you are – you are so much more.

Let's stand together and unite against bullying – it's *dangerous* and can lead to self-harm, severe mental health issues and even suicide. We should all support each other and become 'one'. See the resources section in the back of the book for anti-bullying organizations.

After Virgin, I worked as a receptionist in London for a while and things were fine, but I found that I missed the travel and the flying, so I got a job with Thomson Airways. For the six months of my contract, I had a whale of a time – it's ironic, isn't it, that the budget airline gave me the most fun?

My next flying experience came a couple of years later, when I joined Emirates Airlines at the age of 21 and moved to Dubai to live. I reinvented myself yet again and made lots of new friends. Although many of the locals and managers had a low regard for the English girls generally – they thought we were promiscuous – there really wasn't any bitchiness at Emirates (perhaps because it's such a multicultural organization) and I partied and had a ton of fun.

It was as if I was growing up on my own abroad, I guess. I did that job until my mum got sick and I decided to return to England. I remember looking out of the aeroplane window on the way there, peering down on the clouds and thinking, *Everything's going on down there. I need to be down there. And I want to be known for doing something.*

By then, the bullying was behind me and, as we all know, I did become well known. But little did I realize that fame itself would bring a whole host of other problems.

Racial Abuse

In the village where I grew up, we were the only Asian family, and we were constantly subjected to taunts and racial abuse. We were called Pakis and told to go home. I remember my brothers coming home from school crying because they'd been called names. On one occasion, one of my brothers retaliated and beat up one of his tormentors. The boy's mother came banging on our door, and as soon as my mum opened it and started to speak, the other woman shouted, 'Shut up, you Paki!' Even though my mum was tiny, she stood up to the woman, saying, 'Get the fuck out of here and never, ever cross our family again.'

They left us alone after that, but the racial taunts continued at school. It made me think there must be something wrong with our skin colour and growing up, it gave me a bit of a complex. I just didn't understand it. As I got older, I really embraced being mixed race and being exotic. I loved my skin colour, and I ignored anyone who said anything racist to me, rare though that was. I think I've been quite lucky.

Today I get messages asking me to champion specific Asian causes, and if I can post something on my story or help, I will. But I tend not to bring race into what I do. I'm open to everyone. I don't just talk about being Sri Lankan or Asian – I talk about everybody suffering as one because we are just one. Essentially, our skin colour is *not* who we are. Neither is our name. Nor our age. This is what's been given to us, and people think it's a part of who we are, but it's not. Everybody has the same emotions. Actually, your soul is who you are – everything else is just an add-on.

Surrounding Yourself with the Right People

As a direct result of the bullying in my childhood and later at Virgin, I'm very choosy about who I'm friends with. I find it difficult to trust people, and I now prefer a small circle of close friends rather than a lot of acquaintances. Fortunately, I'm good at picking up on energy, bad vibes and situations, but there have been times in my life when I've ignored this intuition.

After I did *Love Island*, I was constantly appearing in the tabloids, and I started to earn more. I went out most nights, and this lifestyle reached its height after my mum died in 2017; I was partying and drinking a lot, and I was in a toxic relationship at the time as well. I had a hectic social life with a wide circle of 'friends', not all of whom were good to me.

Some were nice to my face, but they would bitch and talk about me behind my back. Others were taking me for a ride because I'm a very giving person – I enjoy being able to help those around me, especially now that I'm experiencing such good fortune – and they took advantage of my generosity.

It wasn't until my little girl passed away that I realized what was important to me: who was talking to me and supporting me; who was checking up on me and consistently looking out for me; who genuinely cared.

I realized that I wanted to be with those people who had an authenticity and a purity about them. I woke up to the fact that some people had not only been taking me for granted, they'd also been abusing my friendship. That's when I started to let go of friendships that were no longer serving me.

I came to realize how important it is to surround yourself with the right sort of people and to let go of the rest. To find your tribe, if you like. As you start vibrating higher, so you start dropping people out around you, whether you do so consciously or not. You start recognizing patterns and traits in people that you didn't see before, and you notice odd or sly behaviour. If ever I get that weird gut feeling, I'll go with whatever's happening and phase people out if necessary.

Naturally, there have been times when I've been very lonely, when I've not had many people around me because I've cut people out, but I've stuck with it. And then I've attracted more like-minded people. It's a process – you must put your trust in it and understand that change isn't scary.

We're all automatically shifting all the time, and sometimes people outgrow each other. It's healthy and even essential for us to blossom. The more I trusted the process, the more I started to attract like-minded people into my life.

❴ MALIN'S MANTRAS ❵

People from your past will resurface – just to test your boundaries and vulnerability. Exes and toxic people in particular smell progress. Issa trap – don't fall into it! Stay solid and protect your peace and spiritual energy.

You just need to have faith in the powers outside of what you can control. It's an interesting one because I think that although we recognize toxicity in lots of ways, we often choose to ignore it by making allowances for someone. We tell ourselves, *Oh, they're going through this.* Or, *That's happening to them right now.* I know this because I've been guilty of doing it in the past. But in my experience, that person knows exactly what they're doing and by making excuses for them, you're just deceiving yourself.

Everyone's on their journey, but don't let their journey affect you if it's doing so negatively. From experience, I'd say that if a friend's always putting you down or has been disloyal and you know they don't have your back, don't be afraid to distance yourself from them.

Toxic friendships can be the worst because these are the people you associate with all the time. And if you're listening to and being surrounded by that negativity, you're going to start to feel your energy drop. You're going to meet that person on their lower level, but really you need to be constantly going up.

A Mantra for Cutting Energy Cords

When I want to sever all connection with a person whose energy no longer serves my best interests, I burn palo santo sticks and say the following mantra:

*'I take back my power by cutting all energy cords
that have formed between myself and any person,
thing or situation that no longer serves me.'*

I also like to burn sage to ritually cleanse my home with smoke, as this welcomes creativity, love and good fortune into our space.

All this is even worse when you're in the public eye. One hundred per cent. Everybody wants a piece of what you've got. You just need to recognize that. I guess it's just the world that we live in. Everyone wants fast fame, quick money, and to succeed. I completely get that, and I do help people who I want to help, whenever I can. That's always been in me, and I don't want it to change. But you need to have boundaries. Setting boundaries is the most important thing.

Trust Your Intuition

Today, I'm good at spotting people's genuine intentions and setting boundaries. In fact, my intuition is amazing – although to be fair, trusting it has taken me some time. I remember when I was in an abusive relationship, I'd feel sick inside – my gut reaction – but I'd let my brain and mind tell me that everything was fine, that everything would be all right again. I was ignoring my intuition.

But gradually, I came to trust my intuition. I listened to it and now I'm very good at obeying it. I use it to help me read the people around me and how they're feeling – if they're in a good mood or if they're not okay. It's important to know this because whatever's happening around you is going to affect you too.

If someone you know is in a bad place, you can help them, of course – that's what friends are for – but it's important to recognize the difference between a person who's mentally low and going through a tough time and one who just wants your attention or to manipulate your relationship.

Spotting an Energy Vampire

If you feel drained and exhausted after meeting up with a particular person, or if you get an uneasy feeling *before* you see them, they may be sapping your energy without giving anything back to you. Here are some of the traits and behaviours you might spot in a so-called 'energy vampire'.

- Self-centredness – they're me, me, me all the time

- A constant need for reassurance

- Negativity

- Bitchiness

- Gossiping – that's low vibing: don't talk to me about someone else if it's bad, because in doing so, you're putting it out to the universe and that's going to come back and bite you on the bum

- A lack of empathy – for example, if you see someone in the street and you feel sorry for them while that person laughs at them, to me, that's disgusting

- Attention-seeking

- Jealousy – when you're climbing high, they don't want to see you succeed. How is that healthy?

- A lack of gratitude

So, if a friend, co-worker or family member is feeding on your emotional energy and you feel bad after spending time with them, or if you sense that they're pretending to have your best interests at heart but aren't genuine, you might be better off without them in your life. We should be vibing high together and lifting each other up.

Malin's Gratitudes

I'm feeling grateful for...

- My guidance and intuition

- Friends coming into my life – Divine timing

- Life growing and expanding with my mindset

- Rebirth. Shedding old skin. New endings, new beginnings

- My heart

Chapter 3

DEVELOPING A POSITIVE BODY IMAGE AND SELF-ACCEPTANCE

Escaping the Pressure to Look a Certain Way

{ MALIN'S MANTRAS }

Yes, I work out. Yes, I eat well. But I'm not striving for my body to look a certain way.

I'm comfortable with aiming to be healthy and strong, and keeping a great mindset.

I've been on a ton of journeys and one of the longest and toughest was learning how to love the skin I'm in. You've all seen me unapologetically modelling underwear, showing off my cellulite and generally being confident in my looks, but in all honesty, getting to the point where I have a positive enough body image to appear in public without my clothes has taken a lot of work over a long period of time.

Recently, I put up an Instagram question asking my followers, 'Who's loving their body at the moment?' More than 90 per cent of respondents said 'No', and that really saddens me. I guess many people are still on that journey to self-acceptance, and I get that. Until a few years ago, I'd have responded 'No' myself.

Eating Disorders

As my mum had been so undernourished during her own childhood, she was determined to raise her family healthily. So, she fed us nutritious meals and restricted our access to junk food. Our packed lunches were so freaking healthy – like grapes, an apple, a brown roll with pâté and gherkins and that's it. I'd be hungry all day until dinner. Then I'd go to my friend's house and scoff my face on sweets and junk food because I knew I wouldn't get it at home.

My mum would hide crisps and chocolate in the washing machine or dryer because she thought we'd never find them there. And in so doing, she was laying the foundations for me to have an unhealthy relationship with food from a young age.

But the real problems with eating disorders began when I was 15. At the start of the summer holidays, I'd gained around a stone in weight and, true to form, my mum bluntly pointed this out to me. So, for the first time in my life, I started to restrict my food intake.

By limiting my eating to 800 calories per day, I lost a stone and a half in weight by the end of the holidays. People were commenting and complimenting me, and from that point on, I just couldn't stop. I was hooked on being thinner.

My best friend and I wanted to be skinny, and we egged each other on. On top of the low-calorie diet, we took laxatives and an over-the-counter herbal slimming tea. However, instead of using one tea bag, as directed, I'd put four bags in one cup, and I knew from the minute I'd taken it that I had five hours for it to go through my system. Then I'd get severe cramps and needed to run to the toilet. I became obsessive about getting the timing right. It got to the stage where I had to take the tea every night to feel light the next day.

The weight was still coming off and I loved the attention my newfound thinness brought me. It's no surprise then that I also developed bulimia at this time. I became super shady, so my family and friends didn't catch on, but, after every meal, I'd go to the toilet and make myself throw up.

Even if I'd eaten something healthy like a salad or food that was well within my restricted calorie allowance, I just wanted it to come out of me. I was also hooked on excessive exercise to stay thin. I remember walking more than a mile to the gym to do two hours of running on the treadmill and then walking back from the gym. I was completely obsessive.

BULIMIA AND ANOREXIA

Beat, an eating disorder charity, estimates that 1.25 million people in the UK have an eating disorder, and around three-quarters of them are women. The good news is that around 70 per cent of bulimia or anorexia sufferers improve considerably or make a full recovery after five to 10 years.

However, that still means that more than a quarter continue to suffer long-term, and you can't get away from the fact that anorexia has the highest mortality rate of any psychiatric disorder – from medical complications associated with the illness as well as suicide.

I'm one of the lucky ones because I came out the other side. But I feel sad that so many people, young girls in particular, are still suffering. Eating disorders are a mental illness. In my case, I felt like I was trapped in my head. It's as if you're in your own prison.

You don't see what other people see. I look at the photos of me competing in Miss England or at the countless body selfies I took on my phone at that time, and my face is so angular – I'm all bones. But at the time I thought I looked fat. I thought I was chunky. That's body dysmorphia.

It's so sad because I remember being inside my head and wondering if I'd have to be on a diet for the rest of my life. I really thought that was how I was going to live my life, weighing myself 10 times a day, taking my scales in my suitcase when I was cabin crew, having a Baskin Robbins ice cream because I knew it would come back up without burning my throat and that it would come out of my mouth quicker because it was cold.

Thank the Lord, I now have a good relationship with food and my body. And you can, too. If you have an eating disorder, you need to take it seriously, and you need to get help: please check out the support services listed in the resources section in the back of the book.

Competing in Pageants

By the time I was 16, I was seriously underweight, and this coincided with my mum suggesting I enter a beauty pageant. She'd seen an advert in the newspaper calling for entrants and she said, 'Malin, you could do this. You could do really well.' We had a big argument about it, and I kept refusing to enter. Finally, she said: 'Come on, Malin. You could win. If you enter, I'll give you £500.' And it was *only* the promise of that bribe that swayed me.

I had zero confidence in my appearance and in what I was about to do. But once I got into it, the glamour of getting my hair extensions and makeup done – so I looked even more different from the goofy kid I used to be – gave me more confidence. Yet, at the same time, having to compete with other girls made me feel less confident. It was a weird contradiction.

What I didn't realize at the time is that there's a big difference between doing it for yourself and loving yourself and doing it because you want to impress people or to gain validation. Back then, I was certainly doing it for the latter.

Today, when I see influencers start up on Instagram, I realize that they might think they look great, but deep down they're insecure because they're doing it for the validation, the likes and the reaction, and not for themselves. There's a fine line between the two.

⭐ VIBING HIGH ⭐

Allow yourself the freedom to make choices that are best for you, nobody else. Let go of society's expectations and take away any comparison to others' appearance. Keep your eyes on your journey. Your journey is valid. *You* are important.

When I was competing in those pageants, you had to look a certain way, be a certain weight; I was also competing against very pretty girls, and that fed my insecurity. Even though I won Miss Bedfordshire and some other regional pageants, such as Miss Professional, and I was in the top 10 finalists for Miss England 2010, I never felt good enough. When you're in those competitions, you always want more.

My mum was so proud of me. There are photos of the Miss England competition where she's standing next to me and beaming. But I was miserable, and the light had gone from my eyes. I weighed around 8 stone, which was very light for my frame (I'm around 11½ stone now), and I had amenorrhoea, where I lost my periods, or they would be very infrequent. I had terrible mood swings, too, which caused me to have lots of arguments with my beautiful mum. I was tired all the time, my hair became lank and listless, and I had constant headaches.

On stage, I stood waiting to be judged by people who held no value in my life. Judged on my appearance alone. I thought that external validation would make me whole. It didn't. It tore me apart. It turned me into a shadow of myself.

Dieting

My obsession with food consumed my entire teenage and early adult life, and I'll never get those years back. I now know that I'm the only one who can complete me; I'm the only one who will get me out of difficulties; and I'm the only one who can give me all the love I need. I now hold the power to build the confidence I didn't have back then, by being kind to myself. I hold the keys to my future. Most importantly, only I can unlock the self-love that I never had.

The pressure to conform to a certain body image in the pageant world certainly contributed to my obsession with being thin and my eating disorders, but in all honesty, my dysfunctional relationship with food continued long after I'd stopped competing.

Once I was cabin crew, I felt the pressure to be slim even more acutely; and in 2012, I also appeared on a TV dating show called *Take Me Out*. With so much pressure to look attractive, it's not surprising that the eating disorders persisted. By that time though, I'd been severely restricting my calorie intake for so long that I just couldn't maintain it full-time. I'd starve myself for a few days and then binge on loads of junk food – all the things I'd been depriving myself of.

And then, because I'd gain a bit of weight, I'd try every diet going. I've been on the Cambridge Diet, the Keto diet, no carbs, fasting, water diets – you name it, I've tried it. What else was there? SlimFast, high-protein diet, the jelly diet, the baby-food diet. Even the bodybuilder diet, where you work out constantly and eat seven meals a day.

I was so desperate to lose weight that I took a prescription-only appetite suppressant that contains ephedrine (speed). While I was cabin crew the drug caused my hands to shake while I was serving coffee. When I think about it now, I'm like, 'Wow, fuck! I put my body through some crazy shit!'

But I've paid the price for this long-term abuse of my body. Even though I eat healthily now, and I take vitamins and supplements, because of the slimming teas and bulimia, I have food intolerances and IBS-like symptoms, and I can't eat any proper food without needing to be close to a toilet. I bloat up a lot too. It's ruined my body for sure.

Resorting to the Knife

Even though I had a bit more of a handle on my eating disorders by the time I appeared on *Love Island* in 2016, I wasn't fully healed. Obviously, I couldn't make myself sick after meals on the show as there were cameras everywhere. So, I really had to limit what I put in my mouth while I was in the villa. I also compulsively observed the cameras and the angle at which they were filming me, so that I looked my slimmest.

So, you can imagine my shock and distress when I came out of the villa and saw the comments made about me in the newspapers. I remember one of the tabloids referring to me as 'the one with the belly on her'. Another described my breasts as 'puppy dog-eared', meaning saggy, and yet another called me chunky.

My fragile self-image couldn't bear these insults, and I immediately booked in for liposuction and a breast uplift. How ridiculous is that? I knew that these are risky procedures and that people have died after having them, but I didn't care. Really.

I had both procedures done at the same time, paid for by a company as a promotional for their cosmetic surgery services. However, rather than being the quick confidence fix I'd hoped for, I found that I wasn't feeling any happier. In fact, I developed complications in one of my breasts and for a long time, I had to endure a seeping wound where the nipple had been re-sited and then become infected. For months afterwards, I was in and out of the doctor's surgery and my breasts were very sensitive.

Yet, a year or so after the surgery, my breasts became sore for an entirely different reason! I'd fallen pregnant and, to be honest, that's what saved me from the vicious cycle of eating disorders.

BODY POSITIVITY

When I was with my ex, he hated me posting photos showing me in my underwear or swimwear. He constantly put down the way I looked and said that nobody wanted to see it. He'd call me a slut, a whore, ugly or fat, and told me that it wasn't appropriate to be showing my body off in that way.

Well, let me clarify here just how *amazing* it feels to be in control of my own body, my own choices, what I wear and what I do. I feel free.

Please don't let *anyone* take away your zest for life, your freedom and your happiness. And don't let anyone control what you wear or how you look.

Here's one of my all-time favourite quotes: 'Your weight may fluctuate – your worth will not.' – @danamercer

The Turning Point

Becoming pregnant with Consy, and then losing her, broke a lot of cycles for me. Having a life growing inside me was a turning point. I'd like to say that I changed immediately, but if I'm completely honest, I did continue to make myself sick a few times in the early stages of the pregnancy. I was so scared of gaining lots of weight. But pretty soon, I realized that I wanted the best for the life growing inside me, and I started eating properly and being healthy.

After the trauma of losing Consy, I never consciously decided to become a positive body-image advocate. Far from it: I was only just getting to grips with my own relationship with food. But weirdly, only a month or so after Consy died – it was International Women's Day, I remember, and I was in Dubai – without really understanding why, I posted a photo of my Caesarian section scar with the caption, 'Let's celebrate who we are!'

★ VIBING HIGH ★

Once you grasp the basics of it, self-love will literally set you free. The rest will follow. Love yourself for everything that you are, and more. Self-love will help you to accept love into your life and bring peace to your soul.

I got the most amazing response to that post, and it inspired me to do more to champion self-love and a positive body image. At that stage, I was still on my own journey in my relationship with my body. Cellulite has always been a thing for me – something I've had to deal with, something I've had to learn to accept – and it's not gonna go anywhere.

But I realized that the more I showed my cellulite, my belly and my rolls, the more it helped other people. And, in so doing, it helped me. I ended up not caring about how my body looked. Everyone's seen it all and I no longer worry that my body doesn't look a certain way – as long as I feel good, and I feel healthy. My attitude has changed completely.

MALIN'S SELF-CARE TIPS

Embrace who you are. Accept your body in all its glory. Here are five things that have helped me to do that:

1. **Fresh air.** Vital for our organs and our mental health, fresh air is amazing! Just get outside whenever you can. Even if it's just for five or 10 minutes, get a change of scenery and get that good nature down you.

2. **Limiting screen time.** Now it's very tempting to just stay on your technology – whether it's a laptop, tablet, or phone – and scroll endlessly. But for your own sanity, it's better to limit your screen time. If you're sat there constantly looking at your phone, your eyes are gonna go all crazy. Your mind is going to get warped into a false reality from watching everybody else's life. It's better to pick up a book, or a notepad, or to do something different.

3. **Good nutrition.** Okay, now's the time to try something new. For instance, I make smoothies every morning. I try and cram all my goodness into one hit: my vitamins, my supplements, my kale – I put it all into a smoothie, and I know I feel a lot better for doing it. So, if you're one of those people who have been snacking on Doritos and a bit of chocolate, and you've been feeling a bit sluggish, get your health out and just start cooking from scratch – trying new things and getting that good shit down you.

4. **Self-development.** Now for me, this is a really, really, good one. I love watching YouTube videos. I love getting things up that I don't know anything about. I love researching topics that I want to learn more about, such as certain spiritual practices, the meaning of symbols or different therapies.

5. **Writing a goal list.** When I get out of bed in the morning, I'll meditate. Then I'll make my bed – even that small task sets us up for the day. So, I've done that, now let's do the next thing... You can write down tasks or goals for you to complete – they can be as simple as brushing your teeth or putting on a face mask or reading part of that book. Your goal list sets you up for the day and gets you going.

Embracing a Healthier Lifestyle

After 10 years of abusing my body, I now know what's right for me, and I also know that moderation works. For example, if I overdo my training and then go a few days without exercising, I don't feel bad any more. Now I opt for exercise because it's good for my body and my mental health and I know I'll come back to it.

If I find I'm beating myself up because I'm having a Red Bull instead of a meal, I can say to myself, *You aren't doing this because you want to be a bit skinnier – you're just having a Red Bull.* I don't punish myself now. I'm able to get out of the blame mindset very quickly.

I don't normally eat crap. I like to have eggs and my smoothie for breakfast, and I eat a healthy lunch and dinner. I try not to eat meat because it makes me feel sluggish and my body doesn't process it well. I'm a pescatarian – I eat a lot of fish. And I do it all for my body. I eat healthily because I want to be healthy, not because I'm trying to lose weight. I'm so done with restrictive diets. I can eat what I want, when I want – provided I'm being good to my body.

★★ Vibing High ★★

When I move my body, I feel empowered, cleansed, and strong. Move *your* body. Energize every cell. Let that energy flow through your veins. Taste the fresh air. You don't have to feel sluggish or demotivated. Get up, get out and make today great.

It's a process. If I've had a stressful week or two and I've had a little cigarette here and there, or maybe skipped a meal, I know that now I'm not doing it to lose weight. However, I do have to remind myself of what living with eating disorders was like for me, and to say, 'Bloody hell, don't go down that route ever again.'

Normally, I eat better without even thinking about it. I disassociate myself from external things. Food isn't who I am. It's not me. Food is there to nourish me and make me grow, to help my mind and stimulate me. So that's how I look at it now. I try to be intuitive about the way I eat. If I'm hungry, I eat. If I get full, I stop. I listen to my body.

It's hard not to attach emotion to eating, but that's exactly what I try to do. I listen to the signals from my stomach. And then I ask what's *really* going on with me at the point when I want to reach for that food or that glass of wine. What's going on in my mind right then. Am I in a good place? Am I in a bad place? Has something just gone wrong?

We're human and we live in a difficult world, so we use coping mechanisms, you know. That's fine, and once you're honest and open with yourself and you understand it, you're at that first port of progress. You're in the process of forming a healthy relationship with food.

Body Confidence

In terms of being confident about how you look and being comfortable in your own skin, that, too, takes time. It's a process. It's about learning to embrace the things you can't change; it's about understanding that it's a part of your genetic makeup, and it's who you are. Sometimes, we'd all like to look like someone else or want a part of our body to look different, but ultimately, that doesn't make us any happier. If anything, chasing something that's never going to happen will make you miserable. So, you should learn how to be you and why you're here on this Earth. Does that make sense?

Self-acceptance is huge. Once you can accept yourself just as you are, it leads to no longer needing validation from other people. In turn, that leads to greater self-worth: a better understanding of what you deserve, better relationships, and so on. It's all interlinked. Knowing that you're safe and secure in yourself and not comparing yourself to people in the workplace or in any other area of your life – it all boils down to self-love.

Although on my social media I now confidently display photographs of my body without filters and completely naturally, to help people and show them a bit of normality – which I wish I'd seen when I was younger – ultimately, you need to help yourself.

Looking at my cellulite might make you feel better about yourself temporarily, but in the long term, if you're focusing your energy on somebody else and something other than yourself, it can't bring results. You need to focus on what's inside of you. The outer always reflects the inner. Only you can achieve true self-love.

★★ VIBING HIGH ★★

This is your reminder that your body is here to serve you. Other people's opinions are not vital to your growth, and validation should come from YOU!

It's important that you figure out the root cause of why you can't accept yourself as you are. There's always a lot more to it – you don't develop eating disorders or lack self-esteem for no reason. Perhaps someone's said something to you, or something has happened to you. For example, in my case, childhood taunts were a trigger. You need to start unravelling all these triggers.

It's a bit like a puzzle and once you find that first piece, you can go from there. You might want to have therapy and talk about it until you understand why you feel as you do. What I know for sure is that you can't love yourself simply by saying an affirmation or thinking positively – it doesn't work that way. It's a process and you need to go deeper.

Whatever's going on in your mind will create whatever's happening in your body and in your environment. At the end of the day, we need to look after what we've got. It's important to nourish your body and be healthy – so your brain can function better, the third eye will open even more, and your mental health will improve.

If you look after your mind, your mind will look after your body and your body will look after your soul. Everything is energy and you need it to be moving correctly and feeling healthy. Your body, your mind and your spirit – you need to have all three in alignment, and then you can be the best version of you.

Malin's Gratitudes

I'm feeling grateful for...

- My lungs, which allow me to run
- My good health
- Life working in the way it does
- My morning routine
- Being in the great outdoors

Chapter 4

FINDING YOUR PURPOSE

Making Your Job Work for You

> ### ❰ MALIN'S MANTRAS ❱
>
> *Accept the situation and move on with a smile.*
>
> *What's meant for you is for you.*
>
> *Less resistance will allow the universe to do the work for you, rather than you doing it yourself.*
>
> *Watch how easily life will flow and work out for you when you understand that everything is meant to be – right at that very moment.*

Subconsciously, I've always known that I was destined to do something with my life. Family and friends comment on how I always fluke it and get what I want, and that's never been truer than in my working life. Not every job has turned out to be right for me in the long run; however, that's a valuable lesson you learn along the way about the manifesting process.

Whatever job I've done – and it's fair to say that I've flitted from job to job – I've always known that I had it in me to do more. At the time, I thought that each new job was what I wanted, but then I got bored of it because it wasn't fulfilling what I really wanted to do in life. Nonetheless, each job I manifested satisfied a need in me and led me to the next step in discovering my purpose.

Becoming a Manifestor

This twisting path towards finding what I was placed on this Earth to do started inauspiciously. While studying for my GCSEs, I worked part-time in a Hollister shop. Now I know what you're thinking, but I wasn't put in a 'model' position, projecting the brand out on the shop floor. No, I went into the 'impact' role – so, basically, folding clothes in the back of the shop.

And that's because I applied for the job before I'd lost the weight and I wasn't considered pretty enough to be a model. Once I'd dropped some weight, they changed my role to model. And then I quit because I found it boring as heck. How funny is that?

My next part-time job, aged 17, earned me some spending money while I was studying for a Diploma in Air Cabin Crew. I was a waitress in a pub, and I loved it. I was always on my feet and rushing about, so that helped me to lose even more weight, which at the time I liked.

I manifested my next job with Virgin Airlines even before I'd finished the diploma course. I don't know where the confidence came from, but I was like, 'Forget this. I don't need to do another year. I can get what I want right now. I can apply to get flying while I'm doing the course.' I was also clear in my mind that I didn't want EasyJet, Thomson or Thomas Cook, the airlines where most newly qualified cabin crew start – I wanted Virgin. And, because I was so strongly set on it, that's how I manifested it.

Obviously, at the time I didn't know what I was doing, but I envisioned myself in that red uniform. I remember when I got the job and told my fellow students, they were like, 'Oh my God, that's the ultimate dream. That's so awesome.' And I was like, 'Boom, I got Virgin. See ya.'

And yet, envisioning alone isn't enough. I wanted the Virgin job and I saw myself in the uniform, but I also prepped hard for the interview. I knew what I had to do to impress. I knew what I needed to look like, too, so I wore my hair in a bun and turned up in a skirt suit wearing red lippy; and I killed the interview. The training was very hard – I failed a few exams and ended up redoing them – but I got the job of my dreams through both manifesting and preparation.

As you now know, it didn't work out with Virgin because of the bullying, and after leaving abruptly, I took a job as a receptionist in the City of London as a stopgap. I commuted every day to the Willis Building, where loads of smart people come in and out, so I had to look the part – it was the same look as for cabin crew, really. The role wasn't demanding, and I spent most of my day scrolling through the *Daily Mail* website on my laptop, looking at the celebs.

I clearly remember thinking, *One day, that will be me. I want to be on there.* Now I'm in the *Daily Mail* almost every day; I can't get out of it! I was so bored in that receptionist job, and I believed there was so much more to me than that, so I applied to Thomson Airways, just to get my foot back in the door of a flying job.

MALIN'S MANIFESTING TIPS

When I think of something that I want to do in the future – motivational speaking, for example – I can see myself doing it; I can see myself on stage in front of thousands, and I feel good about it. I get a burning excitement inside me. It feels good, knowing what I'm going to be doing in the future.

It's important to keep that fire burning, but it needs to come from a good place, not a place of lack. If I were to say, 'Oh, I wish I was like that now, but I don't have it. Why am I not on that stage now?' that's the *opposite* of manifesting. When we overthink what it is that we want, we resist it. If we obsess over something, we block ourselves from getting it.

It's bizarre, but I have such a sense of knowing where my future is, of knowing that I'm going to be okay. I know that I'll speak in front of thousands on stage. I just feel it in my heart. So, I can let go of overthinking and obsessing about it because I know it's going to be there for me.

Once you let go of that control, you allow life to happen for you and things to come into place – this is known as the art of allowing. The universe may offer different paths and options on how to get there; it may keep shuffling them, and there will be lessons along the way. But think of rejection as redirection. It's such a beautiful game that you're playing with the universe.

When I'm manifesting, I envision myself in the situation I want, and then I let go and trust it will come to me at the right time. Ultimately, trusting equals manifesting, and the more you trust, the smoother life becomes.

Moving on Up

I love flying and travelling – in fact, I've always been a traveller. I love to explore new places and cultures. From a young age, I had it in me to want to be somewhere other than where I was right then. I still have an overwhelming urge to visit places I've never been to before and to see what there is to life. I want to explore different cultures and different experiences. So, my six-month contract with Thomson was perfect. However, I don't stick at jobs for too long, do I? Therefore, when the opportunity to explore another one of my dreams came along before my contract was up, I jumped at the chance.

From the youngest age, I'd wanted to be famous and to do television, so when in 2012 a friend applied for what was at the time a hugely popular dating game-show, I went along to the audition with her. I hadn't even applied, but I got the place, and she didn't. The TV show was *Take Me Out* with Paddy McGuinness.

{ MALIN'S MANTRAS }

Make room. Claim it. Don't let anyone get in the way of your dreams and goals. If you're feeling down and losing your vision or motivation, this is your reminder to step back up.

It was a ball of fun making *Take Me Out*. I was clever with the way I played it; because I wanted the airtime, I didn't turn my light off once. I was the girl on the end podium, and I was on the show until the end of the series. The buzz from the show lasted for a while. People must have liked me because I got the most followers of anyone on the show, and so I managed to get bookings for public appearances.

I loved living that kind of lifestyle. I loved the limelight and the attention, which sounds superficial, but at the time, it was so much fun. However, the work dried up a few months after the show aired. I modelled for a while, but that, too, came to an end. Undeterred, I was like, 'Right, I'm ready to fly again. And this time I'm gonna get Emirates.'

The application process for Emirates Airways is lengthy, but I never doubted I'd get the job. There are six different rounds that you need to pass – physical body measurements, maths tests, group assessments, different tasks and interviews – and each time the number of applicants is whittled down. Finally, you have a one-to-one interview. When I found out I'd got the job, I was a bit nervous because it meant moving abroad to Dubai and I'd never lived away from home, but I had the fire in me.

Livin' La Vida Loca

Back in 2013, Dubai wasn't such a popular tourist destination as it is now. I was sad to be leaving my mum and stepdad at the airport, but it was cool to be going abroad to live independently at the age of 21.

The Emirates crew were like family, and I had such a ton of fun in Dubai. I partied a lot; I met cool people; and I made some great friends, some of whom I still see when I go back out there. But all in all, it was a bubble away from the real world.

I was flying long haul and short haul and some places I liked better than others, mainly because of the passengers. When it came to my rota, as ever, I was a good manifestor. I'd get London Heathrow a lot so I could go back home, and I'd get all the good places in the world.

I was part of the Dubai bubble for around a year, but I still didn't feel fulfilled. I knew that although I'd had a lot of fun flying and living abroad for the first time, ultimately, cabin crew wasn't for me. There was something else that I should be doing with my life.

When my mum became ill, I gave up the job without a moment's hesitation. As it was an emergency, thankfully, the visa was cancelled quickly. I quit my rota, sold all my stuff and left. I remember the flight back home; as I lay across three seats and listened to Coldplay's album *Ghost Stories*, I was like, *Shit, what have I done? I'm going back to nothing.*

In fact, I couldn't live back at home with my mum as she was helping my sister, who was going through a tricky time. So, I lived with my best friend's nan while I worked out how I was going to make a living.

I decided to use my skill for applying my makeup, which had drawn countless compliments when I was cabin crew, to set up my own business on Facebook as a makeup artist. I built the business up from scratch and I established a good clientele by working my socks off. I'd travel to clients' houses and could fit in as many as eight a day.

Word spread and I soon got a reputation as the best makeup artist in the area. When I did the makeup for photo shoots, the money was good. Around that time, I paid £9,000 to do a course for professional makeup artists, thinking that would help my business. But I dropped out because I was already at a higher standard than the course – well, that's what I thought, anyway.

In 2016, while I was still a makeup artist, I got the call to do *Love Island* from the same producers who had worked on *Take Me Out*. Boom. Subconsciously, I'd manifested my next appearance on television.

Getting into Alignment

I'd say that I consciously manifested most of my jobs up to and including my appearance on *Love Island*. As I said earlier, I thought that each job was what I wanted at the time, but then I became bored because it wasn't fulfilling what I was really meant to do. I thought I was doing the wrong job, but now I realize that there's no such thing as a mistake. Everything happens in Divine Order and each time, I'm being guided to learn and grow.

It was only after my baby died that my true purpose came to me, and everything aligned. I'd found my niche, my purpose, and the work flew in. My job as a positive body-image advocate, neonatal death charity supporter and a champion for domestic abuse causes aligned with who I was. And once what I did aligned with my purpose, it ceased to feel like work, and it still doesn't.

I never dreamed I could make the sort of money I now earn, and my attitude to work has changed. I don't keep obsessing over my income or where the next assignment is coming from because I don't want my life to be governed by that. Obviously, we need money to survive – and don't get me wrong, it's cool to have it – but ultimately, I ask myself, 'Am I happy with what I'm doing?' And the answer is 'Yes, I frickin' love it.' Really, I love what I do. Knowing that I'm helping even one person – to me that's worth more than anything.

⁺★ VIBING HIGH ⁺★

To attract positive things into your life, start by giving off positive energy. Taking responsibility for the energy you bring means you're in control of the energy you let into your life. Fill your life with people who reciprocate your vibrations.

Once you're aligned with your purpose, your life just flows seamlessly. Obviously, the anxiety occasionally kicks in: *Am I going to get this job? Am I good enough?* We're all human, right. But my favourite quote, 'There is no rejection, there is only redirection', by the writer Matt Haig, makes complete sense to me now. I trust in the universe.

I know it's not easy to let go when our society conditions us to work hard, to focus, to overtire ourselves and stress out to reach our goals. But you know, if you just put your intention out there and let it be – that's the way it happens. It sounds crazy, I know, but it's actually legit. I should know because I've been trialling this stuff for a long time.

Sometimes I find myself angsting over things or trying to make things fit. Then I get 'downloads' in my sleep and I'll wake up the next day and be like, *Whoa, I feel different.* Then I can let go of any worry more easily – I'm so smooth with it now. It's like having certainty, and it's that certainty and trusting that's the key to manifesting.

Good Influences in Your Life

Our minds are the most powerful thing about us, so we must be careful what we expose ourselves and our minds to. We need to watch out for the 'heroes' and 'villains' of the media and choose those who are influencing us in the right way.

Are you seeing too much negativity on your TV and computer screen? Are you following unhealthy influencers online? This is a wake-up call for you to double check. No matter who we are and what we've gone through, if we follow unhealthy influencers or watch unhealthy habits on TV, it will affect us in a negative way.

Here's an example. When I had eating disorders, I'd follow 'fitspo' accounts; I'd follow super lean bodies; I'd follow every diet hack, every diet trick there was. But that just made me feel worse about my own body. I was flooded by all this perfection online. And in fact, it was making things a lot worse for me.

What I'm trying to say to you is take another look at what you're doing, who you're following and what you're bringing into your mind. Because whatever your eyes are registering goes straight into your subconscious mind, without you even realizing it.

So, have a look at your day-to-day life. Are there things that you get triggered by? Are you feeling sad about certain issues – your body image perhaps? Or are you going through grief, loss, domestic violence? Is it the media – are you watching too much news and is it impacting you in a certain way? If so, take stock of what you're consuming.

{ Malin's Mantras }

For every positive change you make in your life, something else also changes for the better. It creates a chain reaction. Don't give up – keep creating good habits and stick with them. This is your sign to carry on.

I'm not gonna name anyone because that's not cool, but I know certain celebrities and influencers who will promote products just for their own gain. They'll speak on topics that they don't believe in, just to get the clout or the attention or the likes, and that's impacted people in a much more negative way than they realize.

If you find yourself following them, get rid. Get yourself some positive influencers who are fighting for change, who are flooding your timeline with the good stuff. Find those influencers who genuinely care about their consumers (consumers being you).

At the end of the day, I understand that it's a job and we all have to sell a product sometimes, but here's what you need to ask yourself about an influencer: Do they genuinely believe in their product? Do they truly care about you? Are they just doing it for money?

The social media world can be a very dark place, and I'm worried for the younger generation in particular. By protecting yourself, and by only watching things that you need to see, and which are good and healthy for your mind, you're also protecting the generations coming after yours. And you're not giving these 'villains' attention that they don't need. Find yourself some heroes and get rid of the villains.

Daydream Believer

I've always been a daydreamer. I'd daydream in class as a little girl, imagining myself in certain situations. As cabin crew I'd look out of the window at the clouds and daydream that I could see myself doing this or that. And then I'd just let it go and get on with life.

And of course, *that's* when it happens. The things that you're not overly attached to come to you easily. Yet the things you really, really want, you don't get that easily because you're putting too much stress on them. When you're tense, and focused only on one outcome, you're stopping yourself from following all the other avenues that the universe might take you down.

Manifesting Your Reality

Subconsciously or consciously, we're all manifesting constantly. So, you need to be careful what you're putting out there. You need to be careful with your thoughts, the way you view yourself, how you view everything around you, how you talk, how you treat money and how you treat other people, because subconsciously or consciously, you're manifesting your reality.

I remember I wanted to be Miss England so badly. I kept saying, 'I want to be Miss England, I want to be Miss England. I want to win. I want to win.' And when I didn't win, I felt as if the whole world was over.

I'd put all my eggs in one basket and was convinced that winning Miss England would be my route to being famous, which was my end goal at the time. With hindsight, I can see that wasn't the way for me and that losing the competition was a blessing in disguise. Being Miss England wasn't aligned with who I am. Alignment is key.

Since my pageant days, I've read and watched a lot about the manifesting process, and I've learned over the years to be more open when manifesting. Now, I might say, 'Universe, direct me in ways that I didn't know were possible. Take me on different journeys, different paths,' because I know that ultimately, I'm going to get there. The journey of life is so exciting, but we're not meant to know exactly what's going on right now. That's cheating. You must trust that the universe has your back.

Signs and Synchronicity

Along with trust, we all need hope. When I was at my lowest point, hope had me. It's hope that you need to get you through the darkness. Hope is in each one of us – we just need to choose to find it. Having hope gives us a glimpse into what could be the future, and it reminds us that things are only temporary, emotions are temporary, and that the dark days won't last forever.

What's always helped me is having the ability to envision a different future. I'm very visual: in my head, my brain and even daydreaming, everything was imagery. I like to work with symbols, which is why vision boards work so well for me.

If you were to look at the homework I did when I was six or seven years old onwards, you'd see it was covered in eyes predominantly, or butterflies and flowers that I'd doodled in the margins. It's weird, but symbols have always held meaning for me. My mum didn't approve when I got my first tattoo, but I loved it. Every tattoo I have has some significance to me from a different point in my life.

Now, I'm open to everything. I still draw symbols and I consciously look out for signs because they help to guide me and reassure me. Signs such as birds, butterflies, feathers, a piece of music that comes on the radio at a random time, meeting certain people, seeing numbers such as 1111 – all of these keep me going because they're a reminder that I'm on the right path: that I'm aligned. The synchronicity of life is freaking crazy.

MAKING A VISION BOARD

Recently, I made a new vision board for myself because I'd ticked off almost all the items on my previous board. As I said earlier, because I like to work with imagery, vision boards have always worked well for me; I was very arty as a child, and without really knowing what I was doing, I made a vision board for my bedroom wall.

For the vision boards I create now, I like to choose images that are symbolic of something or have meaning to me. You can do the same for your boards. Think of the things that you want to come into your life and then select images or messages from magazines, or which you've drawn yourself, that represent those things in your mind.

Next, paste the images haphazardly onto a large sheet of card or paper. Then stick your completed vision board on a wall or prop it somewhere prominent so you can see it every day.

On my latest board, I have photos and other images of the following:

- Oprah (watch this space, I'll be a guest on her show one day).

- Ram Dass, because he just shows me what life is truly about.

- A light coming out of a head, for my soul purpose.

- A wedding dress, which signifies me getting married one day.

- My dream house in Beverly Hills, California.

- My symbol for meditation, the lotus flower.

- Self-help guru Tony Robbins giving a talk – to show that it'll be me on stage one day.

- A phoenix – that's me rising from the ashes.

- The Hollywood sign, because I want to have an impact in the USA.

- The word 'gratitude' in big letters, because I'm so grateful for everything that I *do* have in my life.

- Two faces, to show me my soulmate.

- Growth, which is important to me.

- A butterfly, which shows how far I've come.

- An eagle, which is my spirit animal.

- Gold, to represent abundance.

- The word 'hustle' struck through, which represents not having to hustle to achieve my goals.

- The Ouroborus (an ancient symbol of a serpent with its tail in its mouth), representing the ending of old cycles and the start of new ones – constant rebirth.

You get the gist. Pick anything that has meaning for *you* and stick it on your vision board. Then, glance at the board every day, without being too obsessed with anything on it; those things will come to you when the time is right. I never used to grasp the importance of timing; I wanted results straight away, but it doesn't work like that. You can manifest, but things will only come to you when the time is right.

Abraham-Hicks' teachings tell of a woman who finds a diamond on a walk; you know, there are thousands of people who will have passed that spot, but they didn't find the diamond. It wasn't because that woman was looking for it, but because it was meant to be there for her at that time. She was the one who was always going to spot it, and it was always going to be there for her. We need to remember that, and we need to just trust that the universe has our back.

Malin's Gratitudes

I'm feeling grateful for...

- Life working out the way it has

- My ability to cope

- My work opportunities and the success I've had

- All my guidance

- Being in the flow

Chapter 5

BEING TRUE TO YOURSELF

Surviving the Fickleness of Fame

Although I'd always wanted to be recognized and to be on TV, when fame came knocking, I wasn't actively looking for it. Nor was I prepared for the whirlwind of highs and lows that my sudden celebrity would bring.

In June 2016, I broke up with my boyfriend, a pilot living in Abu Dhabi. I'd flown back into the UK and was at Heathrow Airport when my mobile rang and without any preamble, the caller, a man, asked, 'Malin, are you still single?'

I didn't recognize his voice, so I replied, 'What the heck – how did you get my number?' He was like, 'Come on, Malin, you remember me, I'm the producer of *Take Me Out*! What do you think about doing *Love Island*?'

In truth, I hadn't seen the first series of *Love Island* at that point, but I knew of the show and its enormous popularity. Unhesitatingly, I went, 'Oh my God, I've just become single. I hate men. Yes, let's fucking do it.'

Becoming an Islander

In my head, I viewed the *Love Island* gig as exposure and a bit of fun, and I genuinely wanted to find some love. I was fast-tracked onto the show: I had just one audition, which I smashed, and I was through. I was one of the last contestants to join and there were just three weeks between the audition and heading into the villa.

In that short window of time, I watched the first series and educated myself on it, but I still didn't really know what to expect. I'd never done anything like that before. I was nervous, and I kept thinking, *How am I gonna act? Will I like anyone? What do I do? What do I pack?*

Yet, in all honesty, my attention was mainly focused on dieting and trying to look good before I went in, as I was still in the grip of the eating disorders. I was so worried about my cellulite that I even bought a cellulite machine. My mum, bless her soul, bought me a new wardrobe to wear on the show. But nothing really prepares you for walking into that villa and there being cameras just *everywhere*.

What happened on the series in July 2016 is well documented – I got together with Terry Walsh, and we were a couple. Literally days after I was evicted from the villa, he cheated on me with Emma-Jane – he mugged me off completely. Then, in an unprecedented shock move, the producers brought me back onto the show to confront him publicly about his behaviour. It was explosive viewing at the time.

Although I enjoyed a lot about the villa experience, I was anxious for much of the time too. I was constantly worried about the cameras showing my cellulite, and I was also traumatized by something that had happened to me just before I went into the villa (which I'll share with you in the next chapter).

Today, it feels like I'm describing somebody else when I talk about my *Love Island* days. I hardly recognize myself in that insecure, anxious 23-year-old who entered the villa. I was a different, lost girl back then, but when I'm forced to think about it, I guess it helps me to see just how far I've come in the past five years.

Of course, while you're living in the villa, you've no idea what's happening in the outside world. The producers didn't tell us much, but occasionally they'd say things like, 'Guys, just put it this way, your followers have tripled.' We all got media enquiries left, right and centre, but we didn't really have much of a clue about anything else.

When I came out, I was surprised that people in the street were recognizing me and wanting photos. My first thought was, *Right, okay, so this is something serious. Let's make money.* At that time, I hadn't really figured out what my niche was, so I did the odd paid post and a few things on makeup and beauty.

I'd go to events for the sake of it, to try and get papped, wanting to be in the *Daily Mail* and never quite making it. Or if I did, getting really excited about it. I completely lost sight of who I was.

It's so sad when I look back. Without a niche, I was just trying to follow the crowd, to be a typical islander. But I know now that chasing the crowd and doing what doesn't feel right for you in order to be something you're not, is completely damaging.

I was drinking and partying and attracting the wrong people to me. I was meeting people who were vibing low, I was eating crap, and I was feeling shitty. But I'm testimony to the fact that it's possible to break that vicious cycle.

THE DEMON DRINK

Whenever my life became really, really bad, I found myself turning to alcohol. When things went sour after *Love Island*, when I lost my mum, when I was going through a break-up, I'd drink to numb my pain. I know that for me, alcohol was an escape and a way of getting out of my head temporarily.

The following day I'd be hanging and vibing low. When my baby died, I drank excessively for a week, but then I snapped out of it. In the years since, I've had an on-off relationship with alcohol: going on binges and then going teetotal. But now, before pouring a drink, I ask myself: *Why do I want a drink? Am I celebrating or am I trying to numb out an emotion?*

Using alcohol, or any other substance, to numb an emotion is never gonna work. Now that I know of better ways to heal, I no longer grab a bottle of wine to take the edge off things; I only turn to alcohol if I want to party or have a drink with friends, and if I know I'm in a good place. That's the difference.

To keep my mind feeling great, I've been focusing on not drinking, being on my phone less frequently, and exercising. I know that alcohol is easy to turn to when you want to numb the pain, but trust me, it doesn't help. Try to front up to your worries or problems head on, without that drink.

After *Love Island*

In the months following the screening of my *Love Island* series, I was partying a lot, trying to look glam, trying to be seen with people, in a bid to fit in. I was really badly affected by the vile comments about my body that were printed in the tabloids during the show, and this pushed me to try to look different, to be different. I lost sight of who I was. I was as insecure as anything, and I hadn't found my mission or my purpose. I didn't know whether I was coming or going.

Even though I felt I should be on the up after *Love Island*, I found I was constantly comparing myself to the other contestants, who I believed were faring better than me. I'd continually ask myself *Why didn't I get that? How did they book that job? Why am I not in the press more often?* I was using all my energy to focus on them instead of myself, and it drained me of who I was. The constant comparison was a thief of all joy.

Whatever I did, it was never enough in my eyes. Of course, I was never going to be enough until I told myself that I *was* enough. I've since come to learn that when you feel unaligned with who you are or your purpose, you need to bring it back to basics, to meditate on it and to remember who you are.

You need to separate yourself from your status, because that's not who you are: your job doesn't define you, your friends don't define you, even your name doesn't define you. When it comes to status and others' perception of you, it's not who you are, so don't get lost in that. You need to stay true to yourself. I didn't understand that back then, and I continued to measure myself and my success against other people's – and I found myself lacking.

{ Malin's Mantras }

Don't match anyone else's trash energy. Maintain your own, so you can attract what aligns with you. Keep rising, queens. Don't stoop to them. It's up from here!

After about a year, the work and the fame dried up completely. This coincided with my mum being diagnosed with cancer again in 2017, so I just finished with my management team right there and then. When my mum started her chemo, I cut off my hair and concentrated on supporting her. But I remember thinking, *Shit, what am I doing?*

At around the same time, Xanthe Taylor-Wood, my current agent, was setting up Touch Management. She had Billie Faiers on her books, and she couldn't have been more different than my previous team. She knew I wasn't really getting any work at that time, but she was just there for me. She kept me on the books, and she was patient.

She knew that my mum was dying and that I was going through shit, and she was so supportive, both mentally and emotionally.

Work picked up a bit when I became pregnant in early 2018, as I was offered some deals with pregnancy and baby brands. Nonetheless, Xanthe remained really worried about me as she knew I was in a horrific relationship. She was especially concerned after Sophie Gradon, my friend, and fellow *Love Island* contestant, committed suicide in June 2018.

Sophie was a lovely girl. We were close in the villa, and we kept in touch after the show, even though she lived far away from me. When I heard the news, I was so upset. It particularly bothered me because I knew she'd been struggling and that there were no measures or support in place to prevent such a tragedy. It took the ensuing suicides of Mike Thalassitis in 2019 and Caroline Flack in 2020 before the appropriate support was put in place for contestants of reality television shows after they receive sudden fame.

Chasing Fame

Everyone wants to be famous now. The younger generation think that being famous is the end goal. But honestly, I can tell you from bitter experience that being famous just for the sake of being famous is very damaging. You get thrown in at the deep end and then you're spat out. When I got negative media attention, it really hurt because I kept thinking, *But I'm a nice person, so why?* It was a wake-up call.

Back in the early days, my brothers would take the piss out of me and say, 'You need to stop chasing that fame thing and do something proper.' My stepdad would be like, 'When are you going to get a real job?'

Now, when I say I want to be famous, what I mean is that I want to be well known for what I talk about and the causes I champion. I hide from the paps because I don't want to be part of that tabloid lifestyle. I want to have a private life, and I want to be known for making a change and making a difference.

{ **MALIN'S MANTRAS** }

I'm whole. I'm worthy. I'm worthy of this amazing career. I don't need anyone to complete me. I complete myself.

Recently, I was offered a dream job on a panel show discussing trauma. I thought, *That's so me. I want to do it. It's aligned with me.* Then the producers told me that there would be two other panellists who'd participated in the *Love Island* shows. My body went cold, and I instantly declined the job, even though it was a good brand and good money.

So, let me explain why. I've worked hard to get away from my *Love Island* image. I thought, *I'm not going to be associated with that again because that's not who I am.* And that felt good.

In the months and years following *Love Island*, and before I lost Consy, I'd have accepted that job without hesitation. That's the difference, you see. Now I make decisions based on whether the work is aligned with me. Turning down that job tells the universe: 'I'm being serious about stepping out of this reality TV shit, you know. I'm on a serious journey here.'

Being Grounded

Today, I'm fortunate that 98 per cent of people are lovely to me online and in the press. And, because I'm so comfortable with who I am and what's happened to me, I just ignore the rest or block them. Sadly, though, I was unable to ignore the taunts and abuse I received after my appearance on *Love Island*, and I struggled.

I can understand how people who find themselves in the public eye can commit suicide over trolling. It's horrific. In November 2017, when my mum was in hospital towards the end of her life and had an oxygen tube in her nose, I uploaded a photo of her and someone commented, 'Why don't they unplug her tube already?' That's *so* cruel and hurtful. In fact, I now view it as that person being unwell, but can you imagine reading that about your own mum?

In truth, at the time of her death, my mum was really worried about me, and rightly so. I remember holding her hand when she was in hospital and her looking at me and saying, 'I'm scared to leave you because I'm worried about you. You don't know what you're doing. You're partying all the time and you're so lost. I don't know what you're going to do. That's the only reason I can't leave yet.'

After Mum died, I just gave up trying to be something I wasn't. I surrendered to the universe. Little did I know that, within the year, I'd have to submit further still when my daughter died. Yet it was that complete surrender which eventually led me to my purpose.

At the time, of course, I thought I'd hit rock bottom. Fearing what the tabloids would make of it, and feeling embarrassed, I didn't tell anyone except my closest friends when I took a job as a carer because I needed the money after mum died.

I earned £10 an hour and although it was really hard work, and a lot less glam than going on nights out and trying to get papped, it was humbling, and it made me feel grateful. I looked at this poor paralysed old man every day and I thought, *My body can move and I'm able to function. Look how fucking blessed I am*. Humility and gratitude have been my saving graces ever since.

After the false world of the islanders' party scene, the caring experience brought me back down to earth. It helped me to realize that the core of you is who you are, and nothing else defines you. Not the job, not the money, not the designer bags. That stuff is all bullshit.

MALIN'S GROUNDING PRACTICES

Whenever I feel like I need to be more grounded, I turn to one of these practices:

- Hugging a tree

- Standing barefoot on the grass

- Watering my plants

- Trimming my bonsai tree

- Looking at the flowers, or anything else that's 'earthy'

- Touching my favourite crystals

- Lighting some incense

- Pulling an oracle card

My Reinvention of Self

When you come off a show as big as *Love Island*, it feels horrible when the attention fades. You find yourself in this awful catch-22 where you need to make money, but you know you'll get slated if you get a normal job. You feel as if you've failed, and you feel embarrassed. A part of you still hankers after the limelight, and you desperately try to think of things to keep you in the loop – trying to book anything – but that makes you feel even worse because it's so unaligned with who you are.

Although I found it rewarding to look after someone, I knew that the carer role still wasn't what I was meant to be doing. I felt I had a voice that needed to be heard, and so I kept pushing.

I was lucky. After my baby's death, when I started to share my experiences and I realized that my honesty was helping others, it became clear that I'd found my purpose. My voice could be used for good. I'd been at my lowest point, but once I found my true purpose, my agent Xanthe (who had stuck by me through the worst of times) started booking me good, honest work.

The deals aligned with the causes that are important to me – grief, baby loss, domestic abuse. I was speaking about raw, real things that people don't usually talk about. Xanthe tells me, 'God, Malin, everyone wants to work with you because you're doing things that no one has ever done before. You're stepping into areas that people are scared to touch on.' We laugh about it now because I'm booking major, meaningful jobs instead of doing posts and little promos that don't align with me.

⟨ Malin's Mantras ⟩

Please don't let anyone shame you. If you're sharing your light and putting out your goodness into the world and it doesn't fit in the box others want to keep you in, deflect that shit like a ninja and keep rising.

With the work I'm doing now, I feel more Malin than ever and it's fucking amazing. Being aligned with who you are isn't about what's around you – it's about what's within you. When things aren't aligned with you and you're feeling off balance and anxious inside, life around you will also be out of balance. Once you're aligned, life flows and it's a beautiful process.

Who else can say that they've gone on a TV show viewed by millions, made money in the first year and then let it fall – people forget about you, and then four years later, you're strong as fuck and everyone knows who you are and what you stand for?

I've done it in reverse to the normal way, and I've reinvented myself. It's been a massive rebirth. There's been so much change, but now, because I'm being true to myself, things are fully in alignment and I'm doing the best I've ever done. And the best is still to come, which is amazing.

Malin's Gratitudes

I'm feeling grateful for...

- Always having a roof over my head

- My career

- Being in alignment

- My plants, bonsai and garden

- The friends who don't give up on me

Chapter 6

TAKING BACK CONTROL

Recovering from a Violation of Trust

{ MALIN'S MANTRAS }

With each day, you heal.

*Use every bit of strength to start over and
start believing in yourself again.*

In March 2021 in the UK, the 'date rape' drug GHB, and others like it, were reclassified from Class C to B, meaning those found in unlawful possession of them will face tougher penalties and victims will be better protected from their use. The maximum sentence has been increased from two to five years in prison and/or an unlimited fine. But most importantly, the use of this drug on women and men by sexual predators is now being taken more seriously.

When I read this news, it triggered an uncomfortable memory that I've long fought to suppress. In all honesty, while writing this book, I've had to revisit lots of painful episodes from my past and re-examine them. And although I've often spoken about past traumas in my life to help other women, there's one event that I've never felt able to talk about. Somehow, sharing it on my social media or in the press didn't feel right. I've tried hard to forget this episode but writing this book has brought it back up to the surface and now feels like the right time to talk about it.

Speaking Out

This incident happened before I went on *Love Island*. I'd organized a night out with one of my friends and another friend of hers. We were celebrating and I was staying at my friend's place that night. We had a good time, with quite a few drinks, and then my friend's boyfriend came to pick us up and take us back to her house, which we had to ourselves because her parents were away on holiday. It was the first time I'd met him, and he was not my type of person at all.

We were slightly drunk, but we certainly weren't staggering. I remember arriving at the house and looking through the fridge for food. We spent a little time downstairs, chatting and eating cold pizza, before heading up to bed. I was staying in my friend's bedroom, and she was sleeping in the spare room with her boyfriend. This guy brought me water to take to bed with me, and I can remember drinking some and having the glass next to my bed. The weird thing is, after that it's pretty much a blur.

I fell into a deep sleep, but I woke up in the night to find my friend's boyfriend on top of me. I was conscious, but my body felt like a dead weight. I couldn't move. I felt as if I'd been fucking paralysed, or something. I've never felt like that before. Even when I've been really drunk, my body has never felt numbed like that. Believe me, I know the symptoms of drinking too much alcohol – waking in the night with a dry mouth, needing water and having a thick head – but this was nothing like that.

I was aware of him rolling off me and lying next to me in the bed. It sounds disgusting, I know, but he was lying there finishing himself off. I remember that so, so clearly. It was disgusting. I was feeling so confused, but I remember shouting 'get out' at him, and then he left.

I must have fallen back into a drug-induced stupor – I'm now certain that he'd given me a date rape drug. When I woke up again early the next morning, around 6 a.m., I saw that I'd barricaded the door with a shoe rack and loads of shoes. I don't remember doing that, but I must have done so after he'd left the room.

I saw the mountain of shoes and instantly felt very strange. My intuition told me that something was massively off within my body. I felt violated, but I didn't know how or why. The most intimate part of my body felt different – used.

I ran into my friend's bedroom, and he was lying there with her.

'What happened last night?' I asked.

She's like, 'What do you mean?' But at the same time, she was laughing at me.

I'm like, 'Something happened.'

And she goes, 'Don't be stupid.'

I looked directly at her boyfriend and said, 'Did you come into my room?' He couldn't look at me and didn't say anything.

My friend was still laughing at me, so I said, 'He definitely came into my room.'

I felt sick, disgusted. 'I need to leave,' I said.

I ran out of the room, out of the house and just drove. I didn't know or care if I was still over the drink drive limit. I just had to get away. I didn't feel like myself. I felt groggy, you know – not with it at all.

In Denial

I rang Gemma, my best friend, and told her what had happened. She was like, 'Come here now. Come to mine.' It took about 45 minutes to get there, and the journey was a total blur. I just remember speeding as fast as I could in my Sirocco and feeling really odd.

Once I got to Gemma's, she asked me more about what had happened and then took me back to my house. My mum was in, but I crept past her, went upstairs, and got straight into the shower. I kept scrubbing and scrubbing at myself until I bled. I felt really dirty.

Gemma came upstairs and told me to get dressed as she was taking me to the rape crisis centre. There, they did loads of tests and found this guy's dirty DNA on me. They gave me lots of advice, but I couldn't take in any of the information. I just felt lost. The whole thing seemed surreal to me. I couldn't make sense of it.

ꝶ MALIN'S MANTRAS ꝶ

In that moment when you feel that you can't go on,
realize that there's a lot of life ahead of you that you
have yet to encounter. The darkness is always temporary.

I remember going home that night and shutting myself in my room. I just cried and cried. Eventually, my mum came in and I couldn't help myself, I let it all out. I screamed and cried and clung on to her. She kept saying, 'What's happened? What's wrong? Has someone done something to you?' Even now, I hate to think about how sick I felt as I had to say to my mum, 'I think I've been raped.'

She was furious. She was like, 'Who the fuck did this to my little girl?' She called my stepdad into my room, and my brothers came upstairs too. They made me go to the police and report it.

I found that interview so hard. I felt ashamed. It's ridiculous, I know, but that's exactly how I felt. The police and a forensics team went straight to the house I'd stayed at the night before and collected my underwear and all my stuff, as I'd left in such a hurry with only the clothes I was standing in.

For the next few days, I was in this weird bubble. Totally in denial about what had happened but getting unnerving images and flashbacks from that night of him on top of me. Soon after, I was supposed to appear on *Love Island*, and I just didn't know what to do. My mum was convinced I should still go on the show. 'Don't let anyone ruin this opportunity for you,' she said. 'Don't give them that. You can do this.'

I kept trying to push it to the back of my mind, but it was like the darkest cloud hanging over my head. Finally, as a family, we decided I'd say nothing and go on the show as if it hadn't happened.

A Safe Space

As weird as it may sound, I found it easier to put the whole thing behind me while I was in the villa. It felt like a safe haven. There were cameras everywhere and that made me feel safe; Terry, who I was with in the villa, made me feel safe too. I'm sure there are those who will say, 'If you were that unhappy and traumatized, why would you go on a national TV show?' But little do they know what was going on in my head at the time.

Of course, it was a tough decision to go ahead with it, but my mum was right, I think. I needed to grab this opportunity with both hands – it was what I'd always wanted – and, strangely, I think I needed the distraction.

That's not to say it was straightforward. Far from it. I tried to block out that shit completely, with only partial success. I kept bursting into tears on the show and the producers wanted to know why. But of course, I couldn't tell them. I just tried to put a brave face on it.

Soon after I went into the villa, the rape crisis centre gave my mum and my sister the results of the tests they'd done. We'd agreed a code word for them to use while I was there, to let me know that I wasn't pregnant and that I didn't have any STIs. It was something like, 'Your sister's fine. She's actually having a boy.'

When I got that message, I can't begin to tell you what a huge relief it was. I'd been terrified that he'd given me something. After that, I tried even harder to block out the memory and to forget the awful assault had ever happened.

While I was on the show, my brother wrote me a long letter, saying how proud he was of me for being brave and not letting them win. He told me he was there for me and how sorry he was that I'd had to go through this. As my older brother, he really felt my pain, and he also felt a responsibility to step up because I hadn't known my dad. He finished the letter by saying, 'One day, you'll see, you'll speak about this when you're ready.'

But I just didn't feel I could at the time. I felt so violated. I felt disgusting. It was too raw for me to talk about back then. So, when I came off the show, although the police chased me to follow it up, I dropped the charges.

My brother was like, 'You can't do this. You can't let this guy get away with it.' But I couldn't face the possibility of not being believed. My friend laughing at me and not believing me, and sticking with the guy who had raped me, had really shaken me. I couldn't do it. I was terrified of people finding out and judging me. I wanted to pretend it had never happened.

Post-Traumatic Stress Disorder

The thing with denial is that, at some point, the trauma will resurface. For me, one of the worst aspects of this awful situation was that its after-effects crept into my relationship with Tom Kemp, which began the following year. I did open up to him about the rape, but only because I needed to explain why I had the post-traumatic stress disorder (PTSD) symptoms of nightmares and flashbacks.

Initially, he was interested and supportive, asking a lot of questions. Shockingly, though, some people who knew about the allegation were like, 'You're a fucking liar. You're disgusting.' It made me feel terrible.

Thankfully, it's six years on and the flashbacks and nightmares are rare now. To some extent, my tactic of trying to suppress the memory has worked because I'm only partially aware of what went on that night. I think the universe was protecting me, you know – I'd be a wreck if I could recall every detail of the whole sordid event.

{ **MALIN'S MANTRAS** }

Always be grateful for what triggers you. This indicates what you're not yet free from. Acknowledge it, be aware of it and then work on it. Healing isn't easy. It's a process and part of the very journey you're on now

In truth, I don't think about it too much if I can help it. I know that it happened, and I can't change that. It just goes to show how vulnerable you can be in certain situations, though. That's why I'm so pleased that the UK legislation around date rape drugs has been changed.

Because of that one night, I don't like being out of control – whether that's through alcohol or because of a particular situation, such as when I'm alone with a guy I don't know well. It made me mistrustful of men for a long, long time.

My guard was up totally. In fact, Tom was my only sexual partner for about three years because it's so hard to trust and to be intimate with someone again after something like that. I think such a violation was so alien to me. By doing what he did, I felt that guy had taken away a part of me; taken away a part of my soul, even.

You feel powerless, in the sense that your body has been violated. It's an attack on you. It's your body. Your intimate place – the site of your sacral chakra, seat of your feminine energy. It's as if the Divine part of who you are has been violated.

POSITIVE AFFIRMATIONS

In the years following my awakening, if I ever found myself giving thought and energy to the event I've just described, or any other awful events in my life, I'd use the following affirmations to bolster myself and my self-belief. If you're struggling or feeling unworthy, try repeating these as you look in the mirror in the morning!

- 'I'm willing to love and accept myself.'

- 'I'm willing to love my body for the life it allows me to experience.'

- 'I'm learning to love myself.'

- 'Piece by piece, I accept myself as the whole as my core.'

- 'I'm worthy of happiness, and I'm meant to be a bigger source of joy for the world.'

- 'I'm worthy of love, and I'm loved, because I'm alive.'

- 'I'm more than my thoughts, my pain and past.'

Finding a Good Man

It must be said that I've had some awful experiences with men, including both sexual and domestic abuse. So, it's perhaps understandable that I'm now pretty choosy about which men I allow to get close to me. It takes a lot for me to let my barriers down.

All I ever wanted was to be loved and protected – to feel safe with a guy. I guess the lesson for me was that I had to learn to do that for myself first: to live alone and be my own kind of protector. Now, I find it scary to think about giving that up and relinquishing my independence.

But trusting a lover takes time. I'm pretty good at spotting the warning signs now, and I'm a tough judge of character. If there's the slightest hint of something being off, or if I get that ick feeling at any point, I'm off. Don't get me wrong, I've kissed a few frogs since Tom, but now I'm good at spotting the signs and listening to my intuition and my body's signals. The body doesn't lie.

Anyone who's been through a relationship with a bad guy will be rightly cautious when they start dating again. What I'd say is do it in your own time, at your own pace, on your terms, on your conditions and always trust your intuition.

The other thing that I've learned is that the connection of a beautiful soul with yours is the sacred beginning of a Divine relationship. You're not supposed to go out and find love. Love will find you when you're good and ready.

Getting Help

Until now, I've never spoken publicly about the rape. I've never dealt with it directly either – I've always fought hard for it to go away by not talking about it and burying it deep inside. Even when I've been drunk with friends who are sharing their deepest secrets, I've not shared this one. I regret that now. I wish I'd spoken out sooner, in a way, because suppressing it isn't the answer.

You could say I was lucky, in a twisted way, because the counselling, the retreats, and the help I received after the domestic abuse and losing my mum and Consy indirectly helped me with the trauma of the rape, even though I didn't specifically talk about it.

I also consider myself kind of lucky that the universe helped me by not giving me too many memories of that night; I'd hate to have a full recollection of the event. I believe the universe has given me a glimpse of what happened, but it has protected me because I don't need to know every detail.

That's the explanation that I choose to believe; however, scientifically, a date rape drug is known to make victims sleepy, or sometimes to fall unconscious, and to cause amnesia, so they can't remember events during the period of intoxication.

{ MALIN'S MANTRAS }

Recognize that you're not on your own in this – and that all these feelings are normal. Take this opportunity to recuperate and feel however you need to. Then use it to develop and move forwards. You got this.

My visit to the rape crisis centre and my report of the crime to the police are still on record and, in the UK, there's no time limit on pressing charges. In many ways, I wish I had sought justice at the time – and it's good to know I still could – but I had my reasons for not doing so.

Now, having been through the ordeal of taking Tom to court for assault, I'm not sure I could face going through that again. Like many victims of sexual assault and rape, I'm also just plain frightened that I wouldn't be believed.

I know it sounds absurd, but in my head, I can hear the non-believers like Tom and my former friend saying, 'She's been through so much; she's probably just making this up. Surely she couldn't have gone through that as well.' That's how being a victim of tabloid attack has made my mind work, I'm afraid. Sometimes, it's a curse being in the public eye because you're fair game for abuse and trolling.

Even so, I urge anyone who's been through something like this to seek help and to speak out. There are dedicated and excellent rape counselling services available, and thankfully the police and the justice system are now taking cases involving date rape drugs and non-consensual sex much more seriously.

If you've been sexually assaulted, remember that it was *not* your fault. Sexual violence and sex without consent is a crime, no matter where it happens or who commits it. Please don't be afraid to get help.

You don't have to report the crime to the police if you don't want to – or you can do so at a later date – but it's a good idea to get medical help as soon as possible as you may be at risk of pregnancy or STIs.

As I've said, it was such a relief to me once I got the news that I was clear of those worries.

I understand that overwhelming desire to shower and wash any trace of your attacker off your body – that's exactly what I did – but if you want to press charges, it's best not to wash your body or clothes after the attack, to avoid destroying forensic evidence.

You Matter

For specialist medical attention and sexual violence support in the UK, whether you decide to have a forensic medical examination or not, your first port of call is a sexual assault referral centre, which used to be known as a rape crisis centre. Or you can see your GP, go to A&E or the sexual health unit at a hospital, or call 111. If you prefer, you can visit a contraceptive clinic.

In the UK and the USA there are services that help victims of sexual assault, including Women's Aid, Victim Support and RAIIN; you'll find their contact details in the resources section at the back of the book.

You are important and *you* matter. If you feel as if you're invisible in this world, you're not. These services are there to help you. I see you and I hear you.

Reclaiming My Power

I feel relieved to finally be speaking out about my experience. It's always been a huge worry that someone would find out, and not from me. Now I want to take the power back because I felt powerless at the time.

After the rape, I went through a lot of anger, denial, resentment – at him and at my former friend for not believing me. I felt dirty, violated, used. I couldn't believe this thing had happened to me. *Why did it happen?*

But then, I think I gained some acceptance when I started to deal with the other traumas in my life, and when I had my awakening. The healing journey is a long one, but I can now say, hand on heart, that I have some peace around it.

Most importantly, the truth is finally out in the open, and I feel as if a great weight has been lifted off my shoulders. And I really hope that I'll be able to give other women their voice to speak about it.

I didn't talk about it straight away because I felt embarrassed and was in denial – a common reaction. By understanding the range of emotions that surround the victims of rape and sexual abuse, and by truly listening to them without judgement, we can make it easier for them to speak out.

The #MeToo movement has helped many women to bear witness to their experience of sexual abuse. Their testimonies have helped to reverse a long-standing trend in the media reporting violence against women that often blames the victim and keeps the perpetrator invisible.

Like many of these women, I'm speaking out not because I want to share my inspirational story of how I've overcome being raped. You don't overcome rape. The experience shapes you.

What all victims want is a more open dialogue about consent, sexual assault and date rape drugs – so victims aren't seen as being responsible in some way – and changes to the justice system. The reclassification of the GHB drug shows that their voices are having an impact.

Malin's Gratitudes

I'm feeling grateful for...

- Being heard and believed

- Having the support of close friends and family

- My body, which is my temple

- Having the courage to trust in love again

- Seeing justice for victims of sexual assault

Chapter 7

GETTING TO GRIPS WITH GRIEF

Losing a Parent

> **{ MALIN'S MANTRAS }**
>
> *Whether you've lost your mum or*
> *a child... you're not alone.*

I'm 28 years old and I've lost both my parents. None of my friends' parents have passed away – they're all still with them. It's just me. I feel like the odd one out and, although my friends are supportive, I don't think they can understand what it feels like. It's not their fault – how could they know what it's like to go through this grief, especially at such a young age. The pain of losing your parents, let alone a child, is unimaginable and impossible to explain, but we *need* to speak about it.

Grief is such a taboo topic, and it makes people feel uncomfortable because nobody really knows what happens when you die. Perhaps it's because I've witnessed so much death in my life so far, or perhaps it's down to my spiritual awakening, but I have this sense of knowing and peace in my heart.

As a result, I'm not scared of death. I know that's rare and maybe it sounds a bit weird, but I feel that if we were all more open around the subject of death and dying, it might help us as a society to deal with the dying process and grieving in a better way.

A Nightmare Made Real

My mum's relapse after 15 years in remission came during that strange period after the *Love Island* show, when I was still chasing the islanders' celebrity lifestyle. I'd kind of gotten used to her being healthy and, even though she'd lived on medication and had been in and out of hospital during her remission, so she was never her best self, I'd thought she was safe.

When I heard the news that the cancer had returned, it was like someone had ripped my heart out all over again. I had these little flashbacks to being a kid, when I'd lie awake at night in terror of losing her, and her disappearing into hospital all the time. I instantly got triggered and it all came flooding back.

This time though, I was older – I'd just come off a major TV show and I was in the public eye, so I put on a strong head and told myself, *No, she's gonna be fine. She's gonna be fine.* My logic was that if she'd beaten cancer once, she could do it again. So, I carried on with my life as if all was well.

And in a strange way, my mum behaved as though she was fine too. She had surgery to remove both her breasts, one after the other, together with a treatment plan of chemotherapy and radiotherapy.

Naturally, she lost all her hair after the chemo, but she was remarkably lighthearted about the whole thing.

She liked to make jokes and sarcastic comments about her appearance. In fact, we joked together. One day, I put an egg next to her bald head and went, 'Look, Mum, this is you!' She thought it was hilarious. She was able to laugh at herself and, in the main, to stay positive.

Yet her recovery wasn't as smooth as expected, and when she stopped eating properly because she was having difficulty keeping down food and drink, I was like, 'Okay, that's a bit strange. There's definitely something wrong here.'

The medical professionals kept telling us that it was IBS, but we weren't convinced. This went on for some weeks, until eventually she was given a diagnosis of stage three stomach cancer and told that she didn't have long to live. *What? How could this be true?* It was my worst nightmare made real.

I simply couldn't process the news. My brain was all out of whack, and, in all honesty, I didn't handle the situation well. I didn't know what to do with myself. I was in complete shock and denial over it. I didn't want to believe that my mum was dying. No one wants to believe their mum is going to die. All those nightmares I'd had as a little kid were about to become my reality and I couldn't handle it. I distanced myself from the situation and spiralled into a dark state of depression.

On the surface, it looked like I was unaffected or uncaring because I continued to party, but when I was alone, I cried all the time. I felt so sad and depressed. I can honestly say that this was one of the worst periods of my life because I lost myself, and I knew I was losing my mum – I just couldn't bear the prospect. I felt that there was no reason to be alive. I drank and partied to numb the pain and the only way I could sleep was with the aid of sleeping pills.

Sleep as an Escape

I was first introduced to sleeping pills when I was cabin crew and living in Dubai. It's common practice to take them when you're flying through different time zones and jetlagged all the time. So, I'd take the pills if I needed to sleep during the day before a shift. I soon came to love that feeling of drifting off that they gave me, and I became addicted.

When I was struggling because my mum was ill and dying, I came to rely on sleeping pills entirely. While I was partying but feeling miserable and lonely inside, I'd take three or four sleeping pills with alcohol to numb out the emotions. I'd take them at 8 p.m. so I could fall asleep early. I wanted to sleep for as long as I could, so I didn't have to face the day.

Sleep was my escape, but then I'd wake up feeling drowsy and out of it. Although I was trying to lose myself in sleep, in reality the pills made me feel worse because while I was on them, I wasn't being my true self. I was suppressing the real me. I was in an addictive cycle, and I put up with the horrific side effects of the sleeping pills – dizziness, lightheadedness, headache and gastrointestinal issues such as diarrhoea and nausea.

When I became pregnant, I stopped the sleeping pills immediately. However, I went back on them later, to help me through the grief of losing my baby, and when I was so afraid of being alone at night. At some point in 2020, though, I realized I didn't want to live like that any more. I didn't want to wake up being 'half of me'. I went cold turkey and threw away all the sleeping tablets.

Today, I have a solid bedtime routine. I use room and pillow sprays, particularly lavender oil, and a diffuser with essential oils. I also have a Lumie wake-up clock, which adjusts the light intensity to simulate sunrise and sunset. If I can avoid using an alarm, I will, so that I don't wake up feeling startled and anxious. I let my body be as natural as possible, and that includes its sleep and wake patterns.

Spending Time with Someone Who's Dying

My mum's cancer was very aggressive, and it took just a few months for her condition to deteriorate dramatically. I think it was once she was in the hospice that the reality hit me, and I could no longer deny what was happening to her. I really wanted to spend what little time she had left with her, so we moved her out of the hospice and back home. As a family, we cared for her at the end. I decided to stay downstairs with her in the living room, and I slept next to her on a mattress for the final few weeks of her life.

Those last precious weeks with my mum gave me an opportunity to say to her all the things that I wanted to. I think I apologized; I definitely felt regret for my behaviour as a teenager – not wanting to talk to her, telling her to leave me alone, being too busy, not being at home. I know I cried a lot with her. I also told her that I felt like a failure because I'd gone on *Love Island* thinking it was going to transform my circumstances and yet I still had no stability in my life.

And it pains me to know that my mum left us still worrying about me, wondering what I was going to do with myself and my life. All she wanted was for me to have a good, solid boyfriend, a family and a good job. And, most importantly, to do something I loved.

And that was the problem – she knew I loved being in the limelight, she knew I loved having a platform, and she also knew that there was more to me than just the way I look. I know she'd be so proud of me if she was alive today.

Nothing can prepare us for watching someone we love deteriorating every day as they move closer to death. Yet that was exactly what we siblings did with my mum, even though it was really difficult. Initially, she could only eat small amounts, but as the weeks went by, she couldn't even take water down her throat without being sick.

I think the hardest thing for me was not understanding death and what I was witnessing. I really had to come to terms with watching my mum die, yet it was so abnormal at the age of 25 to witness a parent's death – I thought that I'd see my mum grow old and she'd see me married with a family.

{ MALIN'S MANTRAS }

The best thing to do when you feel overwhelmed is to let go and release control. Trying to control the situation creates resistance and makes it hard for you to see the problem. Step away for a little bit. Let your body get out of fight-or-flight mode so you can think more clearly.

My mum was just getting skinnier and skinnier as the days went by. I remember Googling what it's like when someone dies. As in, how do they die? How do you know what to look out for? How do you know when they're close? When they've died?

It was so messed up. Mum's body was so frail, and her eyes were slowly losing her soul. After all that searching through the internet, I still didn't have a clue what was going on, but my intuition told me she didn't have long left to live.

Watching for the Signs

Of course, no one can put a timeline on dying; you know, my mum survived a month longer than the doctors said she should have, but then she'd always been a fighter. It was almost as if me and my family were counting down the days until she'd die, you know. Between us, we were predicting her passing.

So, I was closely watching for the signs as my brother and I took it in turns to sleep next to her downstairs. I think it was about three days before the end when she started to slowly lose her mind a little and we had to witness these really upsetting psychotic episodes.

In the middle of the night, she'd start screaming, shouting and waving her arms about, and she tried to get out of the bed. On one occasion, she shouted 'Mary, Mary,' as if she could see the Virgin Mary. I was like, 'What the fuck, Mum? What can you see?' We were all brought up as Catholics and my mum was very pious, so perhaps this was a comfort to her, but it freaked me out, I can tell you.

I still cry when I think about my mum's last days. Losing the person that you most want with you in life is so traumatic. They're being taken from you and it's outside of your control – there's nothing you can do about it, so you feel completely helpless.

The day before mum died, she lost consciousness. They say that the last sense to leave a dying person is their hearing and that, right up to the moment of passing, they can still hear their loved ones' words. So, I kept talking to her and comforting her until the very end. Although I was holding her hand as it lay on the bed, it felt like she was drifting away and that I was losing my grip on her.

On the day my mum died, I remember waking up that morning with a sense of knowing that she was going to pass that night. And so, I didn't leave her side at all. I sat right next to her, holding her hand.

I said to my brothers and sister, 'Guys, she's going to go tonight.' In the early hours of the morning, her breathing changed. I'd seen on the internet that this is a typical pattern – just before the final moments, the dying person starts to breathe a bit more heavily. I sat still and I kept listening. I heard her last sighing out-breath and then she was gone. That was it. After all the traumatic build-up to her passing, she was gone, and her body was becoming cold. I actually have no words for that moment.

My mum died at 2:05 a.m. on 25 November. It was the 25th anniversary of my dad's passing and I was 25 years old. You can see why the number 25 is hugely significant for me now and will stick with me forever.

Finding Strength

If you're looking after someone who's going through a terminal illness, or dying, my best advice is to keep some faith. I don't mean in a religious sense, but faith that you'll get through this.

We had about three months with my mum once we'd received the stomach cancer diagnosis. During that time, she had good days and bad. Even though the diagnosis was terminal cancer, we didn't want to admit it or believe it.

So, in addition to keeping faith, my advice to anyone watching over someone who's terminally ill is also to have hope: hope that they're going to be okay – medical miracles do happen. Or hope that they're going to a better place. Or hope that they might last a little bit longer to be with you. It's a beautiful thing. Don't ever lose that hope.

My other bit of advice is to stay strong – and by that, I mean staying strong for you, not for other people. Don't feel that you've got to put on a brave face with your family and friends. Understand that you need to be your own rock. I know that you feel you need to be a rock for other people who are also witnessing this traumatic event, but at the end of the day, it's about you and how you deal with your emotions and your pain. By covering it up, you're leading yourself down a really long road to recovery.

I thought that I had to be strong. I acted brave until eventually I thought, *You know what, I can't do this any more*. And *that*'s when my healing started. My grieving for my mum was delayed – I was in denial about her dying for at least six months, probably more. Once I started grieving for her, so the healing could start.

As humans, we want to put on that brave face constantly and pretend that we're fine. I'm telling you that it's okay not to be fine. And one thing I'll add is that it's okay to feel confused and unprepared. While I was caring for my mum towards the end, I fed her, wiped her mouth, took her to the toilet, bathed her and watched as she disappeared in front of my eyes. Yet in truth, there were times, especially right after the diagnosis, when I didn't want to be around her because I didn't want to face the reality that she was going to leave us.

{ MALIN'S MANTRAS }

'If the only thing you can do right now is survive, do that. Trust that in this difficult time, this is what strength looks like.' – Dhiman

So, I've been there and I'm telling you that these coping mechanisms that we have are normal. Please don't feel guilty or bad about it. It's so easy to put the guilt and the blame on yourself, but we're all different and we all process our different feelings at a different rate, at different times.

The trauma and grief that we go through are different for every single person. Don't compare yourself to anybody else, or to the experiences of friends or acquaintances, because this journey is unique to you and your family. Just do it your own way.

I had very mixed emotions throughout mum's terminal illness and dying process. One day I was fine, the next I was sad. I was aggressive and I was angry; I took things out on my family and my closest friends, and my emotions were all over the place. You just need to go with it, to go with the flow of however you find yourself feeling. Don't let anybody tell you otherwise. Because this is *your* journey. This is the way that you're dealing with it and the way that you're processing it.

THE BIG C

According to the NHS in the UK, one in two people will be diagnosed with cancer in their lifetime. This is such a shocking statistic, but you only have to look at my family to see how many of us are directly affected.

If you feel as if you have no one to speak to, there are many charities out there that can help. They supported my family. The list of support charities is long, so get a personal recommendation or go online and trust your intuition to choose.

Therapy can be amazing, too. Even now, I get PTSD symptoms about being alone. In my head, I have the trauma of seeing my mum's dead body lying in the coffin, among other things, and it's scarring. But therapy, particularly hypnotherapy, has helped me.

The journey to healing after losing someone to cancer or any illness is long and slow, but you have the time. Take everything as it comes, be kind to yourself and don't be too proud to seek help.

Saying Goodbye

Before she died, my mum said that she wanted to be cremated, so we respected that and together, we organized her funeral according to her wishes. She'd always loved seeing me in my cabin crew uniform, looking smart, so I wore a nice suit for her.

Naturally, it was a very tense and emotional day. There were a lot of friends and family present, and I remember getting quite drunk at the wake because I didn't want to feel any more pain. Yet for me, the most memorable part of the day was opening a letter from my mum. She'd written an individual letter to each of her four children, which she said should be opened after the funeral.

When I opened my letter and saw mum's shaky handwriting at the end (she'd got someone to type up the main body of the letter), I could feel her around me. It was so strange and emotional. In the letter, she told me how much she loved me and that she felt sure I'd meet a good man – a Christian – and have a lovely family.

She also told me, among other sweet sentiments, 'You're naturally beautiful. Don't take away your natural beauty by wearing a lot of makeup. You don't need it... Take care of money wisely... Mum just wants you to do the right thing... Be a strong girl....' She'd signed it with love from heaven.

To get that special personal message from my mum after her funeral was so beautiful yet so sad. I just cried, *How can you tell me there's no afterlife? What? I get that letter and that's it? No.* I could feel my mum with me. I went into her bedroom and her body was no longer there but her belongings remained. It's my belief that we leave this Earth, essentially moving from human to non-physical form, but our soul remains.

★★ Vibing High ★★

'Energy never dies. Once energy escapes an expired body, it seeks a new vessel. The soul that adored you can't wait to come back into your life, many times with a similar purpose.' – Dr Carmen Harra PhD

I wanted some sort of confirmation of that from my mum. I craved any form of communication. I became obsessed with trying to hear from her, feel her, see her. And she was sending me signs, which helped to open up my mind to everything around me. The electricity kept flickering, a feather would appear, there would be a mist in the room, and she'd come to me in my dreams. In fact, I dreamed about her so often that I started a dream journal.

We scattered my mum's ashes on Brighton beach on the south coast of England, and I go there occasionally to look at the sea and tune in to her. I also have a few bits and pieces of hers in a memory box that I've kept as sentimental reminders. But I don't need to make it into a shrine to remember her – she's always with me.

Being Reborn

On the day my mum died, I had shivers. In a strange way, I instantly felt as though I'd been reborn. I started to see the world differently and I realized what was important. It's as if I saw myself in a sharper form and I was like, 'Well, life's completely different now.'

Questions that I never used to ask kept coming into my head. Things like, 'What is the universe? What's around me? Why is this happening?' I'd look up and see glitter particles in the air, like weird little bursts of energy. And I could feel my mum's presence all around me.

I also saw signs all the time – white feathers on the floor and lots of birds, especially doves, kites and even eagles. The number alignments and synchronicities also continued and 1111, 1212 and 1313 kept showing up in my life: in the car, on the microwave, on the clock. I didn't understand it all at that point, but it gave me a sense of wonder and a sense of peace and comfort, a knowing that everything was going to be okay.

Nobody told me about the significance of this stuff. It wasn't as if someone had said, '1212 is an angel number', and then I'd looked out for it and seen it. I was as non-spiritual as fuck at that point. To be honest, I simply noticed these odd coincidences and would be like, 'Oh, that's weird.' All I knew for sure was that it gave me a strange feeling inside – I felt peaceful and okay whenever I saw these double numbers and signs.

I remember going to Kew Gardens in London with a friend about a week after my mum died, and I just kept questioning the meaning of life. Then my brain started to get really weird, and I was like, 'There has to be more to life than what we're seeing or what we've been told.' It just came out of nowhere.

In stark contrast to my own newfound spiritual seeking, my sister and my brothers had a strong Catholic faith to sustain them after my mum's passing and through the funeral. The rituals of the Church and them falling to their knees and calling on the Holy Spirit had never made any sense to me, even though I was raised a Catholic.

Once Mum died, it dawned on me that through religion, I'd been looking to an external source to comfort me when in fact all the comfort I needed lay within me. That new truth made sense to me, and it explained why I'd never felt comfortable in my youth trying to follow my mum's faith and practices.

Despite my unexpected rebirth and new knowing, I still felt scared and alone after Mum died. I took to my bed and didn't want to see anybody. I felt as though everything I'd been living up to that point was a lie, and that I'd finally been woken up. I find it hard to explain how, on the one hand, I felt desperate grief and sadness, as if I'd been cracked open, yet on the other, I felt like I'd finally woken up and that I understood what my purpose was here on this Earth – finally, I knew who I was. It was a paradox.

Out of the Darkness

Physically, the trauma of losing my mum triggered an autoimmune response in my body and I developed psoriasis on my scalp and all over my legs. It had developed once before, when I was in a toxic relationship with the pilot in Abu Dhabi; the only other times psoriasis has appeared was after my little girl died and after the break-up with her dad. But, touch wood, I haven't had it since. Clearly, my body manifested an autoimmune response to trauma, on top of the mental anguish I experienced.

I just couldn't escape the sickening feeling that my mum, who had been my rock and my biggest supporter throughout my entire life, was no longer here. The world felt like a scary and lonely place without her. I remember in those weeks following her death, lying in my old bedroom at my mum's house, and I really didn't know what I was going to do with myself. I cried endless tears. I felt so helpless, and I just wanted this torture to be over.

Looking back, I realize that while I was in this dark place, I was tweeting some weird, depressing tweets. Things like, 'Life isn't fair,' 'Why did it happen to me?' and 'What's the point in living?' I think I'd fallen into a victim mentality – a dark rut that I couldn't get out of. On one level, I knew it wasn't helping me at all, but I felt so low, I couldn't stop myself.

People sometimes comment on those negative tweets and on how far I've come since those days; they also ask me how I overcame my victim mentality and how I maintain my positivity. Ultimately, I guess I realized that I had to make a choice. Nobody else could do it for me. I had to get myself out of that state. I was the one who decided to go and buy a book to try and help myself. It was me who started to research therapies. I drew on something deep within me to help myself.

However, I don't underestimate how hard it is to help yourself, especially if you're on medication, for example. What I would say is don't mistake positivity for being smiley all the time. That's not what it is – we all have bad days, even when we're woke.

It's about being self-aware enough to know what works for you – to know how you can best manage those dark days, to know what helps you to get out of the darkness, and to understand that tomorrow is a new day and that you can start over again.

Positivity is about how you manage your thoughts, feelings and emotions – what helps you in that moment in time. Go and get some lavender oil, read a book, take time out to be in nature – whatever you need to do when these feelings arise, when you face that trigger, when you get sad. It's okay to be sad for a while, of course. But then you need to help yourself a bit.

THE GRIEVING PROCESS

Grief is exhausting. It makes you feel so fucking alone, and as if there's no way out. I know, I've been there. But please understand that this world needs you. It needs you to be at your *most* vulnerable for you to grow through the pain. It's when we most want to give up that the magic is about to happen. We don't know it in the moment, but it takes the darkest time for the brightness that's within us all to be unleashed.

I too have cried myself to sleep, had suicidal thoughts and attempts, and experienced ongoing depression; our head is a hard place to live after the loss of a loved one. But I'm here now writing this for you, so you can see that you *can* get through it. Persevere and let the heartache guide you to a better place – because you *will* get there, I promise you.

Please look after yourself and don't feel that you must always be 'brave'. The universe has your back, even when you think it doesn't.

Suppression and Heartache

I met Tom Kemp within a week of my mum's passing. It would be another three months before we started dating properly, and during that time, I continued with my quest for spiritual knowledge. However, once we got together, our new relationship was so intense that I stopped my searching and put all my energies into being 'in love'.

If I'm honest, I didn't have enough time to grieve properly for my mum, and I suppressed my feelings. Instead of grieving, I got caught up in a whirlwind of distraction from the pain – a new relationship, parties, drinking, mixing with the wrong people. These were all part of my coping mechanism. And it was all so bad for me.

On top of everything else, David, my mum's partner throughout her 25 years in the UK, met someone else soon after she died, and they got married six months later. He'd been like a dad to me and had stayed with my mum until the end. But as soon as he remarried, he blocked us all and cut us out of his life. That really hurt and it left us confused, you know. I still can't believe he did that to us while we were grieving.

After losing mum, I'd thought I was completely wrecked and cracked open, but the universe had more tragedy in store for me, with an abusive relationship and the death of my baby daughter to endure before I was finally at the point where I could let the light fill my days and my life could change completely.

Finding Independence

Despite everything, a major positive came out of my mum's death: I was forced to discover my own independence. Right up until she was dying, I was heavily dependent on my mum. It had always been like that. As I said earlier, she'd spoiled me because I was her youngest, her little girl. She'd always felt sorry for me because I hadn't known my dad. She'd been both my mum and my dad when I was growing up. When she died, I was still living at home. I felt lost with work and my career, and I didn't know what to do.

It was a strange realization for me, at the age of 25, a young adult, just how much I'd depended on my mum, both emotionally and to bail me out financially. I was like, *You need to sort yourself out*. Her death forced me to grow up and become more independent. In my heart, I know that if she hadn't died, I'd still be the same, still reliant on her. I had to learn the hard way. Losing her forced me to find myself.

★★ **V**IBING **H**IGH ★★

Holding on to what was will not change what is. Let go and make room for what is meant for you.

To learn the true meaning of life I had to be alone and independent. I like who I am now a million times more than who I was when my mum was alive. That's really sad. I wish I could be the person I am now and still have her in my life, but unfortunately, it doesn't work like that. To grow, I had to have the pain of losing my mum. Sadly, I needed trauma in my life and to be a victim of pain to grow into who I was meant to be.

Dealing with Memories

I still feel my mum close by all the time. I wear her ashes in the form of a necklace virtually every day. I find it hugely comforting to have her so close to me. Actually, the way I came by the necklace is a funny story. When we scattered Mum's ashes, my sister retained some of them and had them made into a gemstone necklace. I was pregnant at the time and didn't give it too much thought.

However, one of my sister's church friends told her that this was a bad thing to do, that Mum's body needed to rest in peace and that she should throw the necklace into the river. *You're not fucking throwing Mum into the water*, I thought.

However, I didn't want to upset my sister, so I offered to throw the necklace into the river for her. I then told her that I wasn't parting with it and begged her to let me keep it. She relented and I've worn it ever since. I freaking love it – I think it's the best thing ever.

Today, I've worked out ways of dealing with my memories, thoughts and grief that feel right for me. As I said earlier, I have a memory box for my mum and one for my little girl. I always wore a ring that Xanthe gave me while Consy was in the incubator, and I only recently took it off because I felt as though I'd moved on – that's now in her box, together with her little doll. When I feel like it, I'll open Mum's box or Consy's box and look through it and it reminds me – it's a nice thing to do.

However, I know I have to live in the present. I think that grief takes you into the past and, for me, depression lies in the past. The future can take me into anxiety but being in the present is where I want to be. I need to train myself more on that one.

Of course, there are still times when I feel sad and miss my mum. Special days like birthdays, anniversaries and Mother's Day are tough for me. I find Christmas especially hard because it has never been the same since Mumma passed. It was always a big family occasion for us all, especially the build-up to Christmas Day.

My childhood memories of Christmas are all so warm, happy and loving. Mum made it so special for us because we were without our dad. With Mum dying at the end of November, Consy being born on 23 December and dying at the end of January, it makes the festive and New Year period even harder for me.

Every year, it's a reminder of how I'm on my own and how much I long for my own family. As I hang the baubles on my Christmas tree, it feels all wrong without my mum being present. But, when I need her the most, she'll always turn up in my dreams. I know she's around me. Now I think she's letting me get on with my life. She's watching me grow, and I think that gives her soul a lot of peace.

Malin's Gratitudes

I'm feeling grateful for...

- Morning meditations

- My ability to help people with their own grief

- My positivity

- Signs from the Divine/angels

- My beautiful necklace

Chapter 8

RETAINING YOUR PERSONAL POWER

Breaking the Cycle of Abuse

Sometimes, life events coincide and conspire against you so that you find yourself in a situation not of your choosing. Unfortunately for me, all the pieces fell into place at the end of 2017, leaving me vulnerable to a toxic relationship that I truly believe I wouldn't have tolerated if my mum had still been alive or if I'd grown up with my dad to show me what to expect from a loving partner and father.

Growing up without a father figure in your life is tough. It distorts your view of men, of how you should be treated. I allowed a lot of nasty pricks into my life because I never had my dad to tell me it wasn't okay. My mum tried her best, but she was ill for a lot of my life and her strength wasn't always in her; and it isn't the same. I clung on to a toxic relationship because I wanted love. I wanted to be loved.

I didn't get it at the time, but now I can definitely say that losing my dad affected me a lot. I've dealt with it, but the absence will always be there – that empty space in my heart. The love, reassurance and protection of a father wasn't there, so I went seeking it through my relationships. And that's the worst possible reason to go into a relationship – looking to be completed. That's when you're open to being manipulated and hurt.

Experiencing Narcissistic Abuse

In November 2017, I met Tom Kemp, a painter and decorator and the man who would turn out to be Consy's dad – and my tormentor. We met at a house party within a week of my mum's death. How's that for timing? I was partying to numb out the pain of losing my mum and I was in a very vulnerable place. I felt I had nothing.

Although we were drawn to each other, I resisted his attentions at first – and believe me, he bombarded me with them: sending me up to 50 texts a day, compliments and gifts. This love bombing eventually got results, and we started seeing each other in February 2018.

With him in my life, I finally felt as though I had someone to hold me up, to look after me. I wanted to be wanted and our relationship became intense very quickly. I thought I'd found the love that I so desperately craved, but things soon turned sour.

Growing up, I'd never witnessed any sort of abuse or violence in our home, so when it started, I didn't really understand what was happening to me. It was a very gradual and weird process that slowly altered the way I behaved and alienated me from my friends and family. Until then, I'd been lively and outgoing – or 'mouthy' as he called it – but these qualities were slowly broken down in me. I became timid, so as not to trigger him.

The abuse started with sly digs and him needling me. He'd call me a 'fat bitch', and then immediately say, 'I'm only joking. You're beautiful.' The insults got worse and more frequent as he preyed on my insecurities. I was spending every single day, every single minute, with him, and I didn't recognize that his words and actions were affecting my self-confidence or see how vulnerable they were making me feel.

If my mum had still been alive, she'd have told me what's what for sure. There would have been somebody in my life to tell me what was going on and to say, 'That's not my little girl.' Sadly, I had no parent around to do that for me.

In the early months, Tom was prone to explosive rages, during which he'd shout and throw my things around. He'd punch walls and smash up furniture in the apartment around me, but at that stage, he didn't touch me. It was terrifying, nonetheless. I'd try to get away, but he'd restrain me, pinning me down so I couldn't leave.

Yet, as quickly as these outbursts came, so they were over, and he'd be sorry. He'd cry and beg for forgiveness, skilfully reeling me back in. At that time, I had no idea that I was in a relationship with a narcissist.

WARNING SIGNS OF NARCISSISTIC ABUSE

Are you concerned that the person you're involved with may be a narcissist? The following are signs that you may be able to spot at the beginning of your relationship:

- You make excuses for their bad behaviour, instead of calling them out

- You let them persuade you to turn your intuitive yes into a no

- In your head, you think their persistence means they're really into you

- You downplay your feelings of anxiety and doubt

- You mistake them wanting you all to themselves for intense love

Sometimes, all we want is to be loved and to have the idealistic version of love that we hold in our heads. I've been there and I've done that. I sacrificed everything else to have that fake feeling of love.

Don't blame yourself if you miss these warning signs because it's so, so easy to do. We can't blame ourselves for what we didn't know at the time. Now you're educated, though, you're not gonna make the same mistake again. See the resources section at the back of the book for services that support victims of narcissistic abuse and other forms of domestic abuse and violence.

I knew that I should leave Tom, but I was so raw after losing my mum that I stayed. Honestly, at that time, I'd rather have had him, even with his temper, than be on my own. I was terrified of the prospect of being alone. I desperately wanted our life together to be nice, to be normal, so I'd make excuses for him and tell myself that everything was fine.

Hooked In

In May 2018, I found out I was pregnant. Tom knew I was trapped and that's when the abuse escalated – he started hitting, punching and kicking me.

I felt as if I was walking on eggshells the whole time, hoping I didn't say or do something to set him off. I never knew what was going to send him into a rage; there were no warning signs. Mind you, I was hypervigilant if he'd been partying and drinking. In fact, when he turned up drunk, I'd refuse to let him into the apartment. But he'd smash down the door and ransack the place. Then he'd leave for a few days – he'd go back to his mum's house. Weirdly, he was a real mummy's boy.

I did try to put a stop to the relationship a few times – I'd block his calls and texts. I think the longest I went without contact with him was a week, but then I always relented. He'd promise to change, saying he'd never hit me again, that he hated himself for hitting me and that it would stop.

Like a fool, I'd believe him and let him back into my life. He'd act okay for a week or so, but then something would happen, and he'd explode again. I booked counselling and he came with me twice, but then decided it was 'a load of shit'.

{ **MALIN'S MANTRAS** }

*Sometimes, you just need to remove people without
warning. We're too grown to explain to others what
they already know – that what they're doing is
wrong. Don't feel bad or guilty for doing so – the
space and energy around you is sacred. We don't
need to waste another moment on explanation.*

To be honest, I was obsessed with Tom at that time. It was like an addiction; I couldn't get him out of my head. I believed that I needed him in my life to feel alive. All this, despite finding out that he was cheating on me with his ex-girlfriend, who was the mother of his two little boys. While he was with me, he even went on a family holiday to Jamaica with her and their sons. Can you believe that? But still I stuck by him. The whole thing was crazy.

Making Excuses

One of the worst incidents took place when I was about six months pregnant. We had an argument and Tom threw me into a wardrobe. I fell on my back and my stomach hit the side of the bed. I was dazed and I sat there on the floor shaking and crying. He just went to bed, and he lay there and cried.

Six Ways that a Narcissist Will Hoover You

'Hoovering' is a form of narcissistic abuse in which the narcissist will try to draw you back into the relationship using lies, emotional blackmail and manipulation.

1. **Pretending that your relationship isn't over.** They continue to message you; they show up at your house; and they act as if everything's normal – so that you come to believe that it really is normal.

2. **Sending gifts.** They send flowers, cards, any gifts in the hope that you'll go back to them.

3. **Admitting their faults.** They try to engage you by apologizing, but really this is just a ploy to get you to speak to them.

4. **Indirect manipulation.** They try to get to you through your friends and family members, asking them to pass on messages.

5. **Declaring love.** They say things like, 'You're my soul mate,' 'I'm in love with you,' 'I'll never meet anyone else like you,' 'You're my real love.' But if their actions don't reflect their words, then it's a load of shit.

6. **Sending random messages and making ghost phone calls.** You receive calls from your ex in which they don't speak, or just hang up; sometimes they leave songs and messages that don't make any sense, just to get your attention. All this is just a ruse to get you back into their arms, where it will be even more painful the next time they hurt you.

A month later, the baby's movements slowed. I really started to panic because she was hardly moving at all. On 23 December 2018, we drove together to the hospital, where the doctors discovered that her heartbeat was irregular. And so, Consy, my baby girl, was delivered by Caesarean section seven weeks premature. She was transferred to the Neonatal Intensive Care Unit at Great Ormond Street Hospital in London, where we stayed in parents' accommodation and I kept a bedside vigil.

I was on my own with Consy a lot. Occasionally, I'd join Tom at his home in Milton Keynes in Buckinghamshire for the night. One evening, we went out for dinner, and he went berserk when I asked someone at the bar for a cigarette. He pushed me and bit my lip, making it bleed.

Shaken, I went back to the hospital, where the staff were clearly worried about me. They wanted to call social services or the family liaison unit, but I was adamant that I'd be okay, and I made excuses for him as usual. I went, 'It's fine, it's nothing. He's good. He's just going through some trouble at the moment.' But I don't think they believed me. That was the first time that his behaviour came out of the shadows and into the open.

The Final Straw

Just four weeks after her dramatic arrival, my baby girl died on 22 January 2019. Tom wasn't with me when she died, but he came and collected me from the hospital. We went back to his mum's house, where his two little boys were waiting for him.

I was left standing at the door while he went in and hugged them, all the time watching to see my reaction. It was as though my heart had been ripped out again – it felt to me like mental cruelty. I left and went to my apartment, where I holed myself up for seven days. I didn't want to see him or speak to him. I just drank every single day.

In the months that followed, although we were still together, we coped with the grief in very different ways. Tom tried to live life as normal, and I didn't see any real sadness in him. I travelled abroad on my own 10 times that year; every month I travelled somewhere new. He hated it, but I just needed to get away from him.

By now, I was starting to gain some recognition and validation for my true work – speaking openly about the grief of losing Mum and Consy, and about suicide, and being a positive body-image advocate. I was booking more jobs, doing photo shoots, having in-depth interviews with national newspapers and magazines, and working with big brands. The more attention I received, the more he hated it.

At the time we met I was grieving and trying to maintain the façade of my post-*Love Island* high-life, and he'd used that to his advantage. As my work life started to turn around, he lost that leverage. He then felt overshadowed by what I did, and he fucking hated it.

⁑ Vibing High ⁑

My journey doesn't define me – it only empowers me to want to raise awareness, and it gives me the passion to help others.

In July 2019, things came to a head. We were out with friends, and I wanted to stay out late while he wanted to go home. We argued in the car on the way back, and as soon as we got to his place, he started throwing me about.

He was spitting at me, choking me and kicking me as I tried to gather up my belongings to leave. He wouldn't let me go. I was bruised all over, and although I didn't realize it at the time, my hand was broken. Next morning, when he'd calmed down, he insisted that I drive him to McDonald's.

I was so scared and still shaking, but I went along with it. I dropped him off, pretending that I'd see him later that day. Instead, I drove straight to the home of my friends Greg and Holly. When he opened the door, Greg went, 'What the fuck, Malin?' He said he wanted to cry when he saw the state of me. He drove me straight to hospital; internal and external bruising, a broken hand and I couldn't move for over a week.

The police were called and that was the first step to me having the courage to leave Tom for good. Yet, I'm sorry to say, there were a couple more twists in the tale before that could happen.

Seeking Help

After the attack, a friend took me to the Bedford Women's Centre to enrol on the Freedom Programme, a 12-week course for victims of domestic abuse. That course helped me a lot. I'd never talked about the abuse with anyone before. I remember sitting there listening to the stories of these other women and not believing that I was like them. I thought, *What the heck am I doing here?*

And yet, there I was in the same boat as these battered women. It changed my mindset a lot. It helped me to understand gaslighting and why I still loved this man while he was doing this to me. I've since become something of an expert on narcissism, and he had all the traits. I thought, *Fuck, I need to help other women.* But first, I had to help myself.

{ MALIN'S MANTRAS }

Never forget that nothing is more powerful than the human spirit. You are resilient. There will be obstacles. There will be doubters. There will be mistakes. But with hard work, there are no limits – every day is a second chance!

Even though I'd promised myself 'never again' after my hand was broken, during August and September 2019 he sent me tons of remorseful and highly convincing messages. I knew better of course, but the gaslighting had got inside my head, and I gave him another chance. Stupidly, I went back with him, albeit secretly, because I was ashamed of my relationship with him, and even though it meant he was in breach of his restraining order.

True to form, he couldn't contain his violence for long. In early September we were parked up in his car in a quiet cul-de-sac, just talking, when he threw some Lucozade in my face. This time, there was no hesitation. I went, 'Get me the fuck out of this car now. I'm leaving.'

Thankfully, someone in the cul-de-sac witnessed this and called the police. Tom finally let me out of the car, and I ran to a nearby supermarket. Visibly shaken, I waited outside for my friend to pick me up. Tom went into the supermarket, bought another drink and, without warning, emptied that over me too, saying, 'You piece of shit. Look what you always fucking do. Look what happened. Look what you make me do.' A young boy saw him do that and he came over to ask if everything was okay.

My friend took me to my apartment, where I inspected the massive bruises on my arm where Tom had grabbed me in the car. I stared into the mirror in the darkness of my apartment, on my own, feeling so alone and lost.

As I looked deep into my own eyes, that was the lowest point, without a shadow of a doubt. Literally, my heart was cracked right open. I felt so empty and as if I didn't have anything any more. I thought, *Who is this girl staring back at me? Who am I?* I went to bed that night not wanting to wake up in the morning. But, at that moment, I also knew that this was it. No more chances, no more contact.

#SpeakOutSilenceHurts

I've been very vocal about my experiences of domestic abuse in the hope that doing so may help just one person feel that they're not alone. It's important that we talk about it – to a family member, a friend, a counsellor, or perhaps a charity – because admitting that something's happening is freeing in itself. Honestly, that's the first step to finding freedom.

We need to break the silence surrounding domestic abuse and gender-based violence. That's why I support Avon's #SpeakOutSilenceHurts campaign in the hope of inspiring people to come forward, and ultimately to save lives.

Two incredible UK charities that helped me so much are Refuge and Women's Aid, both of which support women and children who are victims of domestic and sexual abuse; see their contact information in the resources section at the back of the book. Remember, you're not alone, and you *will* be believed, so #SpeakOut.

If home isn't a safe place for you or someone you know, in the UK, call or share Refuge's freephone 24-hour National Domestic Abuse helpline for immediate support: 0808 2000 247. In the USA, call the National Domestic Violence Hotline: 1.800.799.SAFE (7233) or TTY 1.800.787.3224, or text START to 88788.

#ISeeYou

The Wait for Justice

The following day, the police came to my door, which confused me at first because I hadn't reported the attack. It transpired that the young lad who had come over when I was outside the supermarket to check I was okay had recognized me and reported the incident to the police; several other people had also reported it and given witness statements.

He was charged and sent to prison for two months for breaking his restraining order, and then released. We waited another 10 months for the assault case against him to come to trial and for me to get justice. And the wait was torture. Initially, he pleaded not guilty, so for nearly a year, I faced the spectre of having to meet him in court to give evidence. And while I waited, I knew he was out there and still as unpredictable as ever.

For me, PTSD was a very real thing. At night, I'd get scared by the slightest sound, thinking he was breaking in again. I'd freeze, my heart racing. I even had CCTV set up in my apartment. Something unrelated could take me back to that dark place of fear and violence.

Preparing myself for court was all-consuming and a constant worry. I knew he was trying to fuck with my head, calling me 'a liar with mental health issues' in public before the hearing, but I also felt in my heart that my angels were looking after me, because every time the police rang me about the trial, I'd see 18:18 or 17:17 on my clock. And every time he was going to submit a plea, I happened to be out of the country. The angels were definitely protecting me.

When he changed his plea to guilty at the eleventh hour, I cried with sheer relief. In September 2020, he was sentenced to 10 months in prison for assault occasioning actual bodily harm. I'd finally got justice, and even though he served only three months of his sentence, I was vindicated.

Getting Closure

If you've endured physical and/or emotional abuse in a relationship, right now it might seem impossible to you to envision closure. But one day, you'll be able to look back on it all as a chapter in your life, not the whole story. This is called closure. Now, it doesn't mean that you forget, or even that you forgive your abuser. It also doesn't necessarily mean that you're fully healed.

What it means to many survivors of intimate partner abuse is that they're moving on. They're starting afresh and they're entering a new chapter right here, right now. They're walking themselves into a healthier and safer future.

Closure comes in many different forms. For me, it came when I started to heal. The Freedom Programme, my career taking off, my friends, journalling every day and really writing out those nasty emotions, were all part of that healing process. Immediately after I left Tom and I was on my own, I knew I had to heal, and that the only way to move forwards was to go through the blocks.

Here's how *you* can move forwards and get that closure you deserve:

1. Surround yourself with really good people: healthy friends, healthy relationships – people who treat you in the way you deserve.

2. Reclaim your power and find out who you really are. You need to have that self-love journey and to love yourself as you did before you met the abuser.

3. Invest in your healing journey and realize it's not a quick one, it's a slow process. It took around 18 months for me to go through the healing process and journey of self-discovery, to figure out what I really wanted from life and to realize my worth.

4. Go zero contact – get rid of memories, things that remind you of your abuser. Don't watch TV shows you used to watch together. Get rid of the photos and any other traces of that person because, at the end of the day, the relationship was a lie.

5. Accept that you might never get the answers you want. Questions will linger in your mind: Why did he do that to me? Why wasn't I enough? Was it really abuse – he was nice to me some days? Did he ever love me or was it all a lie? All these questions are normal and part of the healing journey. But you have to come to terms with what's happened without getting the answers.

If you've come out of a toxic relationship, even if it was a year or more ago, and you're still thinking about that person, it's absolutely fine. Closure isn't going to happen overnight – it's a process. Be kind to yourself, look after number one. And do You.

My Journey Back to Me

There were many false starts and setbacks along the way on my journey back to me. As you know, I felt drawn to learn more about the universe and spirituality after my mum died, but even though I'd started researching the esoteric and listening to podcasts, once I was in a relationship with Tom, that thirst for self-knowledge took a back seat.

It wasn't until after his final attack, when I looked myself in the eyes in the mirror and realized that I was completely alone without my parents and my child, that I was cracked wide open, and the light literally started to shine into me.

I went without contact with him for several months and, during that time, I forced myself to live alone as it felt like an important part of my healing journey. I confess I found it so, so hard, but I read a lot of books and I wrote a lot – I journalled the fuck out of situations. I went on a retreat in Bali to heal and I spent my 27th birthday there, growing more aware and slowly remembering who I am.

And I was proud of myself. I was like, *Yeah, Malin, you've done so well. The growth is real.* It was a slow journey of learning how to meditate, to journal and to be kind to myself.

{ **MALIN'S MANTRAS** }

Each day you go without contact with your abuser you heal. Nothing ever comes easily. You need to undo all the conditioning they put you through and step onto the ladder of your own self-belief. Use every bit of strength to start over and start believing.

I spent Christmas 2019 in the USA with my brother and his family. It was good to be with them and to be away from the UK for what would have been my little girl's first birthday on 23 December. I came back for New Year, and, against my better judgement, I let Tom weasel his way into seeing me on New Year's Eve.

But the weird thing was, I found him irritating and repulsive. I had the complete realization that it was finally finished, and I didn't want him any more. I didn't need him. I'd had a taste of being on my own and healing, and that had changed everything for me. It came as such a shock to him and, to be honest, it surprised me. I never looked back.

A New Mindset

Around that time, I discovered Vex King's book *Good Vibes, Good Life*. His words had such an impact on me that I reached out to him to tell him so. To my amazement, he replied and offered me more help and advice. Vex helped me to implement my morning routine – exercise, meditation, journalling. I got to know more about myself, who I truly was, because I'd never connected with myself before.

Rebecca Campbell's book *Light is the New Black* was another favourite at the time, but I also watched a lot of videos and did a lot of soul-searching. I literally 'woke up', and the more I educated myself, the further along I went in my spiritual awakening. Don't get me wrong, I had my down days when I wanted to revert to my old, familiar, self-destructive ways, but I was starting to learn what my soul requires for me to function well. I was learning to live life in love instead of fear.

My mindset around the way I viewed myself just changed. I think that all the self-development work I was doing was taken in by my subconscious and then I'd have these epiphanies, or aha moments. There was an epiphany around friends, in the way that I view life, the way I deal with myself, the things I needed to do. It was just crazy.

I'd been through all that abuse from him and all the shit of the rape and losing my mum and Consy, but the way I look at it now is that it was meant to happen, and I was meant to learn from it.

I think I went through these trials and tribulations because knowing my self-worth was always going to be my steepest learning curve. Now, I'm like, *I know how I should be treated. I know my motherfucking worth. I'm a strong-arsed, independent bitch, and I don't need anyone around me.*

REGAINING TRUST AFTER A BAD RELATIONSHIP

You know I like to keep it real, so I won't lie – this is a tricky one. My experience has been one of abuse and being cheated on a lot, so I had trust issues. I understand that if you've lowered your walls and let a person into your life and they've torn your heart out, that leaves you feeling lost, abused and empty. 'How am I ever going to trust anyone again?' is a natural question.

My answer is this: first, you need to trust yourself. You need to really listen to your intuition and your gut feelings, and then you'll spot any red flags at the start of a new relationship. And the only way to tune in to your intuition is to heal your body, mind and soul so you can be in sync with who you really are. Then you start to vibe high, and that's when you attract cool people into your life – people who are worthy of your time and affection.

Forgiveness plays a part in this. Once you've let go and forgiven both your former partner and yourself, you can start to recognize that not every person is the same as them. You can trust your instincts and go with the flow of life; you'll see how beautiful things can be once you start to trust again.

In all honesty, it still pisses me off that after all he did to me, Tom only served three months in prison and he's now swanning around with his sons and his new baby daughter. But I know that's my ego talking, which is normal. Mentally, all cords are cut – I've no emotion, no feeling about him and no hurt. I've set myself free from it all.

In fact, even though he's never shown any remorse, I've forgiven him. I believe that, like most abusers, that's all he knows, and he doesn't understand how to treat someone better. I guess that he must be hurting inside to inflict that pain on somebody else; so, in order to move on with my life, I've forgiven him. I've learned that holding anger in our heart will only make us vibe low, and that living with resentment is unhealthy.

You need to detach yourself. I'm not gonna lie – it's hard because you feel as though that person's taken a part of you. But to get your soul back, forgiveness is key. Their karma will come to them in its own way. In the meantime, I'm grateful I got out alive. I've learned self-respect, self-worth and courage, and I'll never allow someone to treat me like that again. I don't doubt who I am any more and I'm finally able to start living my best life.

A lot of my strength comes from my mum – I had that in me, thank goodness, because it takes a lot of determination and strength to leave an abusive relationship. Even when I was in the thick of the physical abuse, I managed to get up and live every day.

He'd batter me the day before a photo shoot, and I'd turn up and act like nothing had happened. I don't know how I did that, but something was driving my soul through those days, and that same strength helped me after I'd got out of that scenario and into a life of freedom.

Holding on to Hope

To heal fully, I had to go through a lot of soul-searching; I had to unpick what I believed about myself and why my self-esteem was so low. I had to understand the root cause of finding myself stuck with an abusive narcissist and deep down believing that 'this is what you deserve, Malin'. I did a lot of work on my own, but I also went into therapy, and I truly believe that hypnotherapy saved me.

My mind was full of doubting beliefs, things that people had said to me, and I had to unravel the way I viewed myself. I emptied out my pain and examined where it originated – all the stuff I'd collected and stored in my subconscious as a child and a teenager. I learned to recognize that our minds are not us – they don't determine who we are.

So, I think by unravelling my past and dealing with the elements bit by bit, I managed to empty out all the shitty beliefs I had about myself and to create change. It was a slow process, but step by step, I noticed things around me swapping and changing, because I'd been working hard on rewiring what was going on in my mind.

I know that many victims of domestic abuse find themselves in the situation where they're afraid to or cannot ask for help or support. You must remember that you're not alone and that you have the strength to change your life for the better – and help is there for you when you want it.

When I was in that situation myself, it was hope that got me through. It's been a driving force throughout my whole life. If I hadn't had hope, I probably would have attempted suicide until I succeeded. Having hope gave me a faint light in the darkness, and it was hope that helped me while I was working on myself after I'd escaped the violence. Of course, I had my up days and my down days, but hope helped me to believe that the pain was temporary and that I could do something about it.

Malin's Gratitudes

I'm feeling grateful for...

- Having hope

- My courage and strength

- Freedom to speak my truth

- Love

- My angels

Chapter 9

ALL IN DIVINE ORDER

Getting Pregnant

> **{ MALIN'S MANTRAS }**
>
> *Accept the situation and move on with a smile.*
>
> *What's meant for you is for you.*
>
> *You'll always go through what was set out for you.*
>
> *Today, focus on what is within your control and accept the things that you can't control.*

If I'm entirely honest, finding myself pregnant in May 2018 was the last thing I wanted or needed at that time. I was in a relatively new relationship with a man I hardly knew, and although I thought I was madly in love, there remained a niggling voice of doubt in the back of my mind about him and our future together.

Once in the relationship, Tom's love bombing had cooled, and I'd had a few red flags to his potential for emotional cruelty. Like most narcissists, he was skilled at making me doubt my self-worth.

As I've explained, he constantly disrespected me and then pretended it was a joke. He blamed me for things in my past or outside of my control. He manipulated me to get his own way and would get angry over small or unreasonable things. Somehow, I'd then end up making excuses for him and believing his pleas for forgiveness and his claims that he'd change. Hardly the ideal scenario for starting a family together.

Overcoming My Fears

Add into the mix the fact that my mum had died less than six months earlier and I was still a mess from the loss, and you can understand my misgivings. I didn't know what I was doing with my work and my career, which had been practically non-existent for months. I was partying hard to block out the pain and socializing with a crowd who weren't good or true friends to me. It was not the best time to get pregnant – I didn't feel that my life was in good enough shape to welcome a new baby into my world.

I'm sad to say that another factor in my thinking was how I'd cope with the inevitable physical changes that a pregnancy would bring, as I was still wrestling with poor body-image issues at that point. Hand on heart, I can honestly say that, in those early days, I thought I'd be mad to go through with the pregnancy, given all the adverse circumstances.

In fact, I was so concerned about it all, particularly with potentially being with the wrong person, that I went to see my doctor and booked an appointment for a termination. Tom and my sister were dead against the idea and put a lot of pressure on me to keep the baby. It didn't take me long to have second thoughts; for me to realize that I didn't want to go through with it anyway and that I was excited for this baby.

As soon as I'd made that decision, which was very early on in the pregnancy, I stopped drinking and taking sleeping pills, and I started eating properly – something I hadn't been able to do for the best part of 10 years. At first, the thought of getting fat weirded me out, but then I was like, *Okay, forget it. There's a baby growing inside you. What are you doing?* I began to listen to my body a lot more closely and to feed myself and the baby with whatever was needed. I really got in tune with it all.

MALIN'S SUPER SMOOTHIE

Every morning, I make myself a super smoothie. I put everything in it to give my body a boost of essential vitamins and nutrients. And that's never more important than when you're pregnant and eating for you and your growing baby.

My favourite smoothie recipe is as follows, but you can use any fresh fruit and vegetables and if you like, add recommended pregnancy supplements such as Vitamin D, iron, Vitamin C and calcium.

I blitz banana, berries, oat milk, spinach, sea moss, cacao, spirulina powder and collagen powder. Try it! If you're at all concerned about taking sea moss or spirulina during pregnancy, double check with your GP first.

I also started to address my grief for my mum head-on and in a real way. Weirdly, you could say that my unborn child saved me from going down a really bad path. I had her growing inside me and I knew I had to work harder to do things the right way.

I committed to the relationship with Tom to give the baby the best chance of a stable home and upbringing. Sad to say, once he knew I was determined to give it a proper go for the sake of our baby, his behaviour worsened and the violence that I talked about in the last chapter began.

Textbook Pregnancy

I had no morning sickness and no physical health problems during my pregnancy. Like many expectant mums, I felt tired a lot of the time, my boobs killed me, and I was very hormonal, so I got emotional quite a bit, but I found being pregnant a beautiful feeling.

I had lots of scans, but I can't recall if Tom made it to any of them – if he did, it would only have been one at most. I know for sure that, at the time of my 12-week scan, he was on holiday in Jamaica with his sons and his ex-partner, so I went to the hospital on my own. I was so excited to see our baby, but sad to be doing so for the first time while he was with another woman.

It felt very lonely going through the whole pregnancy pretty much as a single mum, without Tom's undivided support. I really missed my mum at that stage too – I know she would have been a huge help to me throughout the pregnancy and really involved with the baby, so that made me sad. My sister and a few close friends who had children were helpful, and Tom's auntie was lovely to me during the pregnancy – we were close at the time – but otherwise, it often felt like it was just me and that baby.

I cried a lot, especially at night. Once she started moving inside me, especially in the evenings, I found it a huge comfort. She was always very active, kicking and squirming a lot, but for the whole pregnancy

I was torn between *Am I going to be a single parent?* and *Am I going to be with him and try to make it work?* It was constantly up and down, on and off. It was so stressful, which I knew was not good for my growing baby.

A Bad Relationship

The constant threat of an angry outburst or even physical abuse meant I could never fully relax. Whenever I cried, or if there was an argument during which he'd shout at me, spit on me, or push or hit me, I'd freeze, and I could physically feel my stomach clench up. I lived on my nerves the whole time.

I left him on more than one occasion and then he'd wheedle his way back into my life. For the sake of the baby, I'd give him another chance. However, the stress of the increasing rages, threats and violence took their toll on me. My brother in America was so worried about me and my unborn child that he insisted I visit him in Los Angeles for a holiday. In the event, I stayed with him and his family for a month.

{ MALIN'S MANTRAS }

Unconditional love is not unconditional tolerance.
Read that again. Know your worth and don't tolerate
anything less. This is your reminder – in case you're
stuck in something that you don't want to be in.

Away from the constant fear of an angry outburst and the stress, I was able to clear my head and concentrate fully on just being pregnant. It was a respite from the emotional rollercoaster. But Tom wouldn't leave me alone: he was constantly texting and bombarding me with messages. My brother said, 'Malin, you stay away from him.' Good advice – if only I'd listened to it. However, because I'd arranged for an early gender scan and a gender reveal party in November, I had to come back to the UK for that. Stupidly, I felt I should invite Tom, as the father, to the reveal party and, to my surprise, he came.

I was thrilled when I found out I was having a girl. Secretly, I'd wanted a girl all along. Friends and family attended the gender reveal party, which was a lot of fun and a real success. They kept telling me that I looked great after my break in Los Angeles, but I knew straight away that it had been a mistake to invite Tom. Sure enough, we got talking and decided to draw a line under the past and move on. I was so keen to give my baby a good upbringing and for her to have a dad in her life that I overruled all my instincts and took him back.

Emergency Delivery

When I was around 33 weeks pregnant, my baby went from being extremely active to scarcely moving at all. I tried all the things I could think of to get her moving – drinking iced water, jogging around and singing – and she did give a small kick, but that was all. I knew something wasn't right. It felt abnormal – a mother's instinct, I guess. So, I told Tom that he needed to take me to the hospital right away.

He'd been planning to go out on his motocross bike, and he didn't want to cancel it. He thought I was overreacting anyway. He just kept saying, 'No, you're gonna be fine. You're gonna be fine.' The feeling that something was wrong just wouldn't go away, so I persevered until grumpily he agreed to take me to Bedford Hospital to be checked out. He made it clear that I was taking a liberty in asking him.

At the hospital, the doctors did some tests that picked up an irregular heartbeat in the baby, and within 45 minutes of arriving, I was being whisked down to the operating theatre for an emergency Caesarean section. Tom had to put on scrubs so he could join me in theatre. I think that's when he realized the severity of the situation and started holding my hand.

I was panicking, overwhelmed. I screamed out for my mum – she was the only one that I really wanted. It was just not how I'd imagined the birth happening. Eventually, I was given an emergency epidural. As soon as she was delivered, Consy gave a weak cry, but she soon stopped. She weighed just 4lb 8oz. I knew the doctors were resuscitating her, but I only found out later that she'd effectively died for two minutes before they were able to bring her round. To be honest, at the time, I was so high on drugs for the pain that I didn't really know what was going on.

It was clear that the medical professionals at Bedford Hospital didn't really know what the problem was. My baby was transferred to Luton and Dunstable Hospital, but they didn't know what was wrong either, so she was then whisked up to Great Ormond Street Hospital for Children in London.

I'd followed my baby in an ambulance to Luton and Dunstable Hospital and answered lots of questions, but it was clear to me that the staff were none the wiser. So, dosed up on morphine and against medical advice, I discharged myself so I could follow Consy to Great Ormond Street, where she was fighting for her life in the Neonatal Intensive Care Unit (NICU). There was no way I wasn't going to be with her, no way.

Calling on My Inner Strength

From the outset, I'd felt overwhelmed by this unplanned pregnancy, but in a strange, surreal sort of way, I thought, *maybe it's a sign – maybe I've been given my own family*, which had been my mum's wish for me. I thought it might have been a blessing.

Looking back, I'm amazed that I found the strength to get through the pregnancy with all that went on with Tom. He systematically went about degrading me until I felt like I was nothing, stripping away the layers of my already fragile sense of self-worth.

{ MALIN'S MANTRAS }

When the universe tests me, I remember
who I am. I take a breath and let
it go. All is well in my world.

He was such a bastard to me that I ended up not knowing what I wanted or who I was. But keeping myself healthy and safe for my baby became my goal. I focused on making sure I ate well, so both the baby and me got the nutrients we needed, and that I got plenty of sleep, so she could develop well. As I've said, the term of the pregnancy itself was smooth, without complications. The only thing that wasn't smooth was the relationship with her dad, which made this a highly stressful period in my life.

To me, it's clear that the constant stress caused by being in such an unstable relationship is what caused Consy not to grow properly. We did genetic testing after the postmortem and this showed that Tom's and my genes were incompatible. It's a rare mismatch, but at the time, the Great Ormond Street specialists told us that she just had a very weak heart.

Without a shadow of a doubt, if I hadn't been pregnant, I'd have left Tom sooner. I wouldn't have stayed with him. Yet, once I committed to the pregnancy, I was living for the baby, and I found the strength from deep inside to make decisions based on what I thought was best for her.

My commitment was total. I put my doubts about the relationship to one side, and I knew what I had to do: I went cold turkey on the drinking and the partying, and I tuned in to my body so I could do everything possible for my baby's wellbeing. I drew on the same strength that had got my mum through an early life of poverty and three cancers. I always knew I had that in me, and I needed it through this pregnancy one million per cent.

There were moments during the worst of the abuse when I questioned why I'd gone through with the pregnancy at all. And yet, when I looked into Consy's big dark-brown eyes, I knew that I was in the company of a very old soul and that she was here on this Earth to teach me an important lesson. Of course, her message and her reason for being here, albeit briefly, didn't become clear to me until sometime later.

The Universe Has Your Back

When we're in the depths of a difficult situation, or life isn't panning out in the way we'd hoped, it's understandable to feel angry or cheated. Yet, once I came to the realization that the universe always has our best interests at heart and will always serve us well, it was easier for me to accept that sometimes, not getting what we want is a gift.

I truly believe that guidance from the universe is our higher self, and that wisdom is always within us. So, even though we talk of the universe as being outside us, the universe is actually *inside* us; I know that sounds very weird.

Let me put it another way. I think that all the time we spend seeking answers externally, we're forgetting to look inside ourselves: to our heart, our mind, our body, our intuition, our inner guidance system. When we learn to tune in to that, we then understand that everything that happens to us happens *for* us. The universe itself is putting us through this process to get us to where we need to be.

Sometimes these experiences seem unfair, and you think *why, why, why?* But they're actually happening *for* you, not to you. You're being redirected. When you're in the midst of it all, it feels like a struggle, but it helps to look at it differently and to understand that you need to let it go. Even now, after all the work I do on myself, I still get disappointed sometimes or try to stay in control of situations. But I tell myself, *Come on, Malin. It's not meant to be*, and I'll give myself a day or so and then let it go. It takes practice.

★ VIBING HIGH ★

Everything's working in my favour, even when it doesn't seem like it. I'll keep believing. I'll keep trusting the process. I won't be discouraged by circumstances or challenges. I'm guided by faith and driven by hope. My vision is clear. I'll stay strong.

I think you can either fall victim to the pain of a situation or you can use that pain to expand who you are. You need to allow trust in that process and that can be very difficult. In any scenario — the guy you want doesn't want you, for example — you need to just let it be: if it's meant to happen, it'll happen. It's hard at the time because the physical body also gets involved — and that affects your emotions, your personality, your health. You really need to count it out. It still happens to me, but now I switch myself out of it.

So, to sum it up: learn to trust the universe. And by that, I mean learn to trust and listen to yourself, because the universe lies within you. Let go of whatever attachment you have to a specific outcome, in the sure knowledge that the universe has your back, and that sometimes not getting what you think you want is better for you.

Malin's Gratitudes

I'm feeling grateful for...

- The blessing of having had a life growing inside me

- My trust in the universe

- Being able to find strength, even in adversity

- My fighting spirit

- My full night's sleep

I'LL ALWAYS BE HER MUMMY

Losing a Baby

{ MALIN'S MANTRAS }

*Life can be so cruel. It can be unfair, and it can
make us wonder why things must happen to us.*

*As easy as it is to stay in a victim mentality, remind
yourself that you're not a victim but a survivor.*

When we arrived at Great Ormond Street Hospital, Consy was in an open incubator in her own little ward. It was the first time I'd seen her properly. I thought she was beautiful – there was so much purity in that face. It broke my heart to see how fragile she was.

She was wired up to even more monitors and we weren't allowed to hold her, but we were able to touch her and stroke her and even change her nappy. To be honest, I was so frightened of hurting her, I didn't even want to do that, so I never got that bonding experience.

In that first 24 hours, the doctors and nurses weren't giving much away. They wanted to do more tests, but they seemed adamant that she had a weak heart. It was touch and go. Exhausted, Tom and I went back to the emergency parents' accommodation that the hospital had provided, where we had to share a single bed with a mattress like cardboard.

The trouble was, I had a fresh C-section wound that was still bleeding, and I could scarcely move. I had to lie on top of Tom in a certain way to feel even remotely comfortable. We didn't have anything with us – our friends brought us clothes and toiletries.

An Emotional Rollercoaster

I woke up early the next morning after a fitful night, feeling sick with worry. It was awful. I just didn't know what to do with myself. As soon as Tom woke up, I was like, 'We need to go, we need to go now.' And then we rushed to the hospital to sit by Consy's side, watching the heart-rate monitor for hours on end. Tired, not eating, just grabbing the odd coffee. It was hellish.

I remember waking up on Christmas Day and feeling so, so depressed. Just two days had passed since her birth, but Consy's traumatic arrival felt like an eternity ago. The Great Ormond Street staff were kind – they gave us a little gift and cards for her, but it was the weirdest feeling. I remember looking at her and thinking, *This isn't how it's meant to be.*

She looked so small and so ill, but despite that, I was very sure that she was going to be okay. 'She's still alive,' I reasoned. You don't expect the worst to happen – I didn't think it would happen to me.

After a few days, we were transferred to permanent accommodation, which was a tiny bedsit with a little kitchen. Even though I was still in a wheelchair, we fell into a sort of routine: we'd sit in the ward with Consy for most of the day; friends would come and visit her; we'd do some food shopping; we'd cook, sleep, and then start all over again. And the longer we stayed, the more intense it became. We were constantly going to and fro between the hospital and the bedsit. That was all our lives consisted of at that time.

We set up a WhatsApp group for family and friends and sent updates each day: one minute the message was upbeat, and she was doing fine, while the next, she didn't have long to live. It was such an emotional rollercoaster. On four separate occasions, the staff told us that she wasn't going to make it, but each time, she showed signs of getting better and we thought she'd pull through.

It was emotionally and physically draining. Our hopes were raised one day and dashed the next. That constant state of being hopeful and then disappointed was exhausting. Eventually, I had to let go and trust in the universe and God's plan.

At 4lb 8oz, Consy was too small to be operated on, so her life was out of our hands. The best thing I felt I could do for her, apart from love and pray for her, was to express my breast milk to help build up her strength. Every few hours I'd pump my milk into the machine, and it was then fed to Consy through a drip; some days she could take a little bit, other days she couldn't.

For much of the time, Consy was heavily sedated, but there were times when she was awake and alert. I'd lean into her incubator and gently tell her, 'Mummy is here,' and she would search for me. She definitely recognized my voice. I loved it when her big brown eyes were open, and we had that connection.

⦃ MALIN'S MANTRAS ⦄

I know that when there is darkness,
there always comes a light.

One evening, the doctors called us in for a chat. They told us that she wasn't looking good. I just cried and cried. I just didn't know how to act, how to be. I fell asleep with the phone in my hand in case someone needed to reach us in the night. Next morning, she'd rallied and the cycle of sitting and waiting started over again.

All this was taking its toll and by the third week, I was left on my own for long periods. When Tom did spend time with me, we'd have arguments, which made the whole situation so much worse. His behaviour was just one more stress to deal with at an awful time.

Losing the Fight

After four weeks in the NICU, Consy caught a virus, which proved too much for her heart to take. I'd gone to stay with Tom in Milton Keynes the night before, but I had this uncanny urge to return to the hospital. He didn't want to come back with me, so I drove there in his car on my own.

It was 22 January, and the doctors told me they needed to change Consy's tube. As I sat watching, suddenly all the machines started beeping and dinging and doctors and nurses came rushing from everywhere to her side. She'd stopped breathing.

The doctors did CPR for 45 minutes, trying to resuscitate her. They told me to leave; I refused – how could I leave my baby? But I did move to the other end of the room. In my head, I can still hear them saying: 'Five, four, three, check.' I felt completely helpless.

When a nurse came over and said, 'I'm so sorry,' bizarrely I remember looking at the time and then I just screamed. I can't explain it, but I think it was as if the raw pain was escaping from me. It was like an empty scream for something – I don't know what it was.

The staff dressed her up and put her in a crib in a little bereavement room and asked me if I wanted to hold her. I was like, 'What the fuck? Why are you trying to give her to me now?' I was holding so much anger inside me. Did I want to hold my dead baby when I couldn't hold her while she was alive? It just felt so wrong, and I couldn't bring myself to pick her up. I was there all on my own. I pulled my hoodie up over my face and I remember it was soaking wet with my tears.

They'd called Tom and he was like, 'I've got to get the train back. I'm coming.' I just didn't know what to do with myself. I was looking at Consy when my best friend arrived. And then Tom got there. I looked at him and I just wanted to get away from him and to get out of there. I felt so angry and resentful. It was all so unreal.

Despite feeling dazed and numb, we had paperwork to do, and Tom had to sign the permission forms for the postmortem. I know that the same evening we had to pack up our stuff from the bedsit we'd been staying in, but it all passed in a blur.

We drove back to Tom's place. It was snowing that day and I remember staring out the window at the snowflakes and I didn't know how I'd got there. I didn't know what I was thinking, what I was doing, because I'd left the hospital with no baby after being there for four weeks. I was a mum without a baby.

When we got to his house, I couldn't bear to see him cuddling his two little boys – it was like a dagger in my heart – so I left him and drove to his auntie's house with tears streaming down my face. She was kind and let me stay the night. Then I moved into the apartment that I'd rented for me and Consy.

While we'd been staying in the hospital, I'd known on some intuitive level that I needed to get my own place – it was clear by then that Tom wasn't going to be around much. Ironically, I was finishing off the application form for the landlord while sitting in the ward beside Consy and telling her, 'Hey girl, I'm just setting up our Royal Mail postal redirection. Don't worry, it's going to be me and you,' when the alarms started sounding in the NICU.

Talking About Baby Loss

When my little girl passed away, all I wanted to do was speak about her. But my friends and support network didn't always know how to approach the topic, and many felt like they were walking on eggshells around me.

I had a lot of friends, but some were there for a good time rather than for when things go wrong. I can count on one hand the people who talked to me and checked up on me after I lost Consy. It teaches you who your real friends are. I understand that people don't know what to say and feel uncomfortable. To my mind, the only way this can change is by having those difficult conversations, raising awareness, and normalizing speaking about baby loss.

So many women carry shame, guilt or embarrassment, or feelings of inadequacy, after miscarriage and baby loss – they feel responsible in some way, and they stay silent. That's why I talk about it, in the hope that I can reach somebody who feels that way.

Don't suffer in silence about the biggest and most awful thing that has happened in your life. Be kind to yourself in your grief and do what's best for you. And by that, I mean be selfish: put yourself first. Also, while you're in the midst of these overwhelming feelings and emotions, try to hold on to the thought that there is a light at the end of the tunnel. See the resources section at the back of the book for services that offer support for baby loss.

In Limbo

Still in shock, the next day we went to Camden registry office in London to simultaneously register Consy's birth and her death. How sad is that? It was a horrendous responsibility for any parent to have to fulfil.

Once I got back from London, I just locked myself away in my new apartment. The reality of Consy's death had started to sink in, and I was inconsolable. I drank solidly from morning to night for almost a week, just to try and numb the pain. A few friends visited me, and Tom tried too, but I refused to see him. I didn't leave my bed; I lay there just racking my brain for reasons why I should carry on living.

I had to use every bit of strength that I had left to get myself back on my feet. I couldn't carry on in that way, and I certainly didn't want to repeat the self-pitying phase I'd been through after my mum's death the previous year.

{ MALIN'S MANTRA }

*A person can simultaneously embody the
power of being a survivor and make space
for the grief of having been a victim.*

Deep inside, beneath the pain, I knew that I didn't want to waste Consy's precious life. I thought about what my mum had been through – growing up in the slums of Sri Lanka, raising four kids on her own, and the beautiful life that she made for us – and I couldn't let those two lives count for nothing.

Sometimes, when you're going through that trauma and those extreme emotions, you've just got to be strong and carry on. Obviously, it wasn't all plain sailing – believe me, I had plenty of bad days, but then I'd pick myself back up and get on.

I thought I'd been broken wide open after my mum died, but it was nothing compared to the way I was cracked apart when my daughter passed away. I bared my soul and surrendered myself entirely to the universe, saying, 'What's my purpose?'

I'd put my spiritual seeking on hold after starting my relationship with Tom, but I knew that there was a path ahead of me that I needed to explore. I also knew that there was no more going back in terms of my spirituality. I just needed to get through my baby girl's funeral and then I could start to find the answers and the spiritual teachers I needed.

THE HEALING POWER OF TEARS

For a time, I think I just had to be low, and be sad and go through all the emotions, instead of trying to cover them up or suppress them with medication, alcohol, partying, friends — you know, masking the truth by staying busy and occupied all the time. It was only once I was on my own that I really started to cry.

Because I'd met Tom at the time of my mum's death, I'd never really got a chance to grieve properly. After Consy died, when I was truly on my own, I let myself cry, especially at night. I cried a lot in 2020, during lockdown. It felt so good to do so. Never underestimate the power of your tears to help you to heal.

Consy's Funeral

When Consy died, she didn't look like my baby girl. She was full of fluid, poor little thing, and I think that contributed to me not wanting to hold her at the time. The thing is, I'd then gone to see her in the morgue, and she looked beautiful again. It was a bit weird because she had the little hole from where the tube had been, but that was to be expected.

So, when I agreed to see her one final time at the funeral directors, it was a shock because she looked absolutely awful. Of course, she'd been through a postmortem, but it just wasn't her. It was horrible. I wish I hadn't seen her like that.

Although I was feeling stronger, I wasn't yet in any fit state to organize my daughter's funeral. So, Tom's auntie made all the arrangements and my sister Emma helped. It was held at St Mary's Church in the village of Woburn in Bedfordshire, where Tom's grandma was buried. In fact, we'd given Consy his grandmother's name as a middle name – Consy Gloria – so it was fitting that her little coffin was going to be placed in the grave together with Tom's grandma. I thought that was a nice touch.

Everyone wore white and 20 white doves were released into the sky as well. We also had a live singer who sang my mum's favourite song, which was beautiful and really moving. But despite the close friends and family at the service and graveside, I just felt so lonely. Tom was very cold towards me – he didn't even hold my hand. The biggest support I received came from my mum, who I could feel pulling me through the day. She was around me throughout and I felt her protecting me.

At the wake Tom's remoteness continued. When he saw me having a drink and a cigarette, he came over and said really aggressively, 'What you doing that for?' – even at my own daughter's funeral he was trying to control and intimidate me. It was horrible. He was checking on me the whole time and being really hostile towards me.

On the night of Consy's funeral, I went to a friend's house and slept on my own, feeling desperately lonely and sad. The next morning, Tom came round, but by then, I knew for sure that it was never going to work between us, and that I had to get away.

My daughter wasn't with us for very long but look what good has come of her life. This little girl taught me so much, and it's thanks to her that I found the courage to leave Tom. I had several false starts when it came to leaving him, as you well know, but the day of the funeral crystallized my thoughts and it was a turning point in the relationship.

DEALING WITH PAINFUL REMINDERS

The truth is, I don't believe I'll ever entirely get over losing my child. At the time, I just learned how to deal with different triggers at different times. I had a system I used to keep my strength up. I blocked myself from seeing pregnant people online – and back then, there seemed to be a lot of celebrities and friends having babies on my timeline.

I reminded myself that I would be a mum again at some point and that all these feelings are normal. Most importantly, I told myself that these feelings are temporary – I have the power to choose to turn my pain into purpose.

If you, too, feel that certain things make you sad and constant reminders of your loss bring you back to an all-time low of pain, then understand that this is normal. We are normal. Me, Malin, I'm normal. You are normal. Do whatever you need to do to survive your heartache and do not feel selfish for this. You are your priority. If you've been affected by the death of a baby, see the resources section at the back of the book for charities that offer support.

Getting Back on My Feet

Although Tom and I were still together, on and off, I spent much of the remainder of 2019 travelling. I took myself to Dubai, the Greek island of Santorini and Spain and twice I travelled to Bali for a retreat, in June and October. As I explained, he hated me being away, and while I was travelling, he loved to send me abusive emails. If I blocked him, he found some other way to reach me.

Bali turned out to be a spiritual home for me, in a sense. I had my very own *Eat, Pray, Love* moment. Have you read the book or seen the film? Yeah, that was me, searching for my soul. All the troubles in my life seemed a million miles away while I was in Bali with like-minded people.

Yet, it was a moment during my stay in Dubai, only a month or so after Consy had died, that had the biggest impact on my life. Friday 8 March 2019 – International Women's Day – was the first time I'd put on my bikini since before I'd given birth.

I looked at myself in the mirror and thought, *Fuck, that's weird. I don't look the same any more.* I was surrounded by loads of young, slim, hip girls – in fact, I used to be one of them when I was cabin crew living in Dubai, and I too had been consumed by my appearance. But I thought, *Now, let me change the narrative.*

{ MALIN'S MANTRAS }

Let your trials, your sorrows, your pain and your losses transform you into more and more of yourself.

I'd carried something so beautiful inside of me, so why should I slave away trying to conform to a stereotypical image of what was attractive? Since losing Consy, I'd become comfortable with myself and with my body as it was.

I posted a photo of me in my bikini with the comment: 'Happy International Women's Day... I'm out here in Dubai and thought I'd share a pic of my postpartum body with you. Here you can see my loose skin and the pouch where my scar is from my emergency C-section. My saggy boobs also, which had milk in them! I'm so proud to say my beautiful baby came out of me, and this is what I'm left with. No baby, just this beautiful scar to remind me. Each body is beautiful. No matter what you look like. All our bodies have a story to tell.'

I couldn't get over the huge response that post received. Knowing that it had helped so many people, I just carried on and started talking about other major traumas that had happened in my life. I wanted to talk about the shit that no one else wanted to talk about. It flowed naturally from me, and I just didn't care any more. Once you hit a brick wall as hard as losing your baby, you no longer care about other people's opinions of you. I wanted to be a lightworker who brings light into people's worlds.

In all honesty, my social media platforms became almost like an online diary for me, in which I'd write out my thoughts and my feelings. It was like therapy. At the same time, talking about the issues in my life prompted thousands of messages each week from people who were either needing help or reaching out to say, 'Thank you for telling your story. It's helped me.'

I found it overwhelmingly uplifting to know that I was using my platform to help others and to raise awareness about difficult issues, and that I was having an impact. I realized that I didn't have to conform. I didn't have to get validation from other people. I wanted other women and men to experience what I was feeling because it's so liberating to feel free within yourself.

Making Sense of Tragedy

Shortly after Consy's death, I was taken into hospital with sepsis and a kidney infection – probably the result of my intensive drinking bout after her passing. In fact, it was around Valentine's Day, because I remember Tom had cut my face during an argument. He didn't come to visit me once during the week that I was kept in hospital. I was alone with my thoughts.

There was nothing I could do; I just had to lie there. So, I ordered a large painting online – it was of an angelic figure; she had wings, but you couldn't see her face. I asked the nurses to put this painting in front of my bed, and for days, I just stared at it. The thing is, it felt to me as if it was my own daughter, Consy, watching over me and, at that moment, I knew deep down that there was a reason for her passing. I'd found a way to process the pain and make sense of what had happened.

I know it sounds messed up, but I knew one hundred per cent that if Consy had lived, I'd always have been tied to Tom. Even if he'd been a distant father, he would have been in our lives somehow and that would have been horrible.

If Consy had lived, I wouldn't have grown. I wouldn't be helping the people that I'm helping. I definitely wouldn't be me. Even though I'd give anything for her to be here and to be okay, look at what I'm doing now and what I've achieved. The knowledge that some good has come from her life here on Earth, however brief, is a great comfort to me.

CYCLES OF LIFE

Each time I've loved someone or have been in love, I've had that person taken from me. So, when I say that everything's temporary, I mean that this is what our cycle here on Earth is about. We come and we go. Someone leaves and new people come into our life, and perhaps they then go too – it's all part of the journey.

What I've learned and what's helped me a lot is to appreciate and live in the present moment, while recognizing that what's happened to me in the past is always going to be a part of who I am.

That's not to say that there aren't times when I miss her and feel sad – of course there are. Birthdays, anniversaries, Christmas and Mother's Day: I can't lie – those days are the toughest for me. But I draw on an inner strength that all the women in my family possess. My mum fought cancer; baby Consy should have died on several occasions, but she fought and fought, and I'm so proud of her for that. That was my mum in her, and I've got that in me.

So yes, I have dark days, but I can pick myself back up again. I thought there would never be a day when I'd wake up and not think about Consy, but there is, because now I think of her when I want to. I have my memory box, and that's all I need.

I'm grateful that although Consy was only in my life for a short period, she made such an impact. She was a beautiful blessing. Despite not being able to hold her, when I looked into her deep brown eyes, there was a connection there, and those moments are precious to me. The day before she died, she opened her eyes one last time, and it was like looking into her soul. I had a sense of knowing that we had a karmic connection.

It was as if she was saying, 'Come on, Mum, you've got this. You know I wasn't meant to be here for a long time. I came to teach you something.' She was such an old soul, and her eyes had such a story to tell. Recognizing that soul contract gave me a confirmation that everything happens for a reason.

Obviously, I do sometimes wonder what she'd have been like if she'd lived. She'd be nearly three now. What would she have looked like? Would she have had the same carefree personality traits as me? And would she one day have become obsessed with the moon and the stars and had a love of cheese and olives and racing cars, like her mum? I guess I'll never know.

I do have a recurring dream in which a little girl with long dark hair and tanned skin is holding my mum's hand. I can't see their faces but I'm pretty sure it's them, and that soothes me. I always wake up in complete peace after that dream. I can still feel sad when I see young families out and about, especially if they have a little girl about the age that Consy would be. I'll always be her mummy.

Malin's Gratitudes

I'm feeling grateful for...

- The blessing of having Consy in my life, however briefly

- Karmic connections

- Understanding that everything is temporary

- My daily morning meditation

- Living mindfully in the present

Chapter 11

MOVING TOWARDS THE LIGHT

Getting Out of a Dark Hole

{ MALIN'S MANTRAS }

Always reach out if you're in need of help.

Don't hold back – it's good to offload.

Throughout my life, my go-to coping strategy in times of low mood, depression and trauma has been sleep. During my late teens and early twenties, I napped a lot during the day and went to bed early. It was a way of making the time pass more quickly. Whenever I was in a weird place emotionally, I'd sleep. It was as if my body knew what to do better than I did.

Wrestling with Depression

We usually think of depression as something that affects adults, but as a teenager, I quite often had low moods. I can't say I was depressed back then, but I certainly had periods of feeling down and nervous. The bullying that I faced at school caused me to feel sad and anxious, for sure, and as I explained, it even led to me pulling out my hair in clumps. But apart from that, I don't really know why I had these dark episodes because I grew up in such a loving home.

By the time I got to my twenties, though, and my mum was diagnosed with cancer for the second time, sad to say, I found out what true depression was all about. Again, I resorted to sleep to avoid as much of the day as possible. When I was awake, I cried a lot.

In fact, I cried every day, and my mum hadn't even died at that time. I think I had this sense of knowing that I was going to lose her, and there was nothing I could do about it. I felt completely powerless and so I couldn't get out of bed, and I couldn't get out of the dark pit I found myself in.

The Conflicting Feelings of Depression

Everyone has slightly different experiences of the black dog, but for me, depression and anxiety mean being scared and tired at the same time. It's being afraid of failure but having no urge to be productive. It's wanting friends but not wanting to socialize. It's wanting to be alone but not wanting to be lonely. It's feeling everything at once and then feeling numb.

That sense of helplessness was the hardest thing for me. But I also felt remorse and regret for what I could have done better as a teenager, in terms of my relationship with my mum. I kept beating myself up about the way I'd behaved. Mainly, though, I was scared because I didn't know what to do when she went. I just couldn't imagine life without her. The thought of being alone made me so sad and so afraid.

And to be perfectly honest, her diagnosis couldn't have come at a worse time. It was a year after *Love Island*, my money had dried up, my self-esteem was low, and I was already feeling vulnerable. Things hadn't panned out in the way I'd hoped after the show, and I wasn't going where I wanted to go. Yet I was very much in denial about this and still living a false party lifestyle. Inwardly I told myself, *So, that didn't work out. Great. But what am I going to do now? I have no stability. Soon I won't have a home or anyone to look after me.* I lived in massive fear, despite the bravado and cool exterior.

My Saving Grace

I can understand why most people might think that the most depressing period of my life was after I lost my little girl, but strangely, that's not the case. Obviously, I was devastated, and I was grieving, but after Consy, I had a fight in me to press on with my life. I think she pushed me in a sense and helped me to avoid the slump of despair and depression.

No, the worst period of depression came after my mum died the previous year. Really. I felt so depressed, and I couldn't find a way out. *Why me?* ran through my head all the time. I was stuck in victim mode for a long time. Thankfully, my spiritual awakening was almost instantaneous after my mum died, and it saved me. If it hadn't happened at that time, I probably would have committed suicide.

I was lucky that my curiosity about all the weird signs, symbols and coincidences I was being shown was just enough to keep my mind busy and away from the hopelessness that I felt. Even though I was grieving, upset and depressed, that new spiritual interest gave me a glimmer of curiosity and kept my mind questioning what life was about.

⁑ Vibing High ⁑

Reflecting. Realizing. Always do what's best for you and never let anyone get in the way of that. Focus on your intuition and nothing can go wrong. If you ever doubt something, there's a reason for that.

When I started dating Tom in February 2018, three months after mum's passing, I was still depressed and grieving. I'd met him so soon after I'd lost her, and as I explained earlier, I know that I was with him in large part because I didn't want to be alone and scared any more.

On top of that, I was completely numbing the pain with the partying. It was purely a way to escape, and it allowed me to be in denial about finding myself alone in this world. I think I was depressed during that whole period, to be honest, because I never addressed the grief or fixed my doubts about the relationship properly. The root causes of my fear, loneliness and sadness were still there.

At that time, my depression manifested in familiar ways. I looked for distractions – alcohol and partying. If I wasn't distracted, I slept as much as I could because I didn't want time to weigh heavy on my hands; I took sleeping tablets. I wasn't really seeing my real friends – which suited Tom, of course – just the faux friends of the party scene. I'd avoid social situations unless it was to get drunk.

I had no drive – I lacked the motivation to do anything, and I felt tired all the time. I didn't really take care of my appearance or look after myself. I turned to food for comfort. I remember I'd go to McDonald's on my own and eat lots of fast food in the car. Emotional eating, a million per cent. I'd even sit for hours in my car outside McDonald's watching Netflix on my phone. That's so sad, isn't it?

Dealing with Intrusive Thoughts

The behaviour I've just described started before Mum had even died and continued until I fell pregnant with Consy, so I was in that destructive pattern for more than six months. Once I discovered I was pregnant, I was forced to clean up my act and focus on my health and that of my unborn child.

However, looking back, I probably should have reached out for help at that point, because the depression didn't go away – it was merely supplanted and masked by the severe anxiety and symptoms of obsessive-compulsive disorder (OCD) I developed during my pregnancy.

These symptoms took a sinister turn after Consy's dramatic birth and subsequent emergency transfer to Great Ormond Street Hospital. I confess that while my baby was lying helplessly in her incubator, I was troubled by the most horrific and upsetting thoughts. Stuff that didn't even resonate with who I am as a person.

I couldn't work out how or why such awful things could come into my head, and I was too ashamed of my own fucked-up thinking to tell anyone about it. Sometimes, I'd look at her and, unbidden, I'd find myself thinking, *Why don't I just kill you? You're going to die anyway.* The weirdest, sickest shit, you know.

I really thought I was losing my mind, and I was scared. All I wanted was to banish these thoughts and quieten my chaotic mind. I went online and researched what it meant to have them and discovered that the link between anxiety and OCD and intrusive thoughts is well documented, and that the whole situation can be made worse by the hormone imbalances of pregnancy.

Given all the traumatic stuff I'd been through and was still facing, combined with the hormones, the anxiety about Tom and the fear of violence, and Consy being at Great Ormond Street, it's no wonder that I was having such mad, weird thoughts.

So, I now understood why these thoughts were randomly coming into my head. But how could I deal with them? I just wanted them to stop. I ordered a book online and had it delivered to the hospital. It was Fearne Cotton's *Quiet,* and I read it in short bursts while I sat next to Consy's incubator – I'm afraid I couldn't concentrate for long because my priority and my obsession was watching over her.

To be honest, I think I was asking too much to think I could quieten my mind completely at such a stressful time, but this book did undoubtedly help me. I came to understand that the thoughts weren't me. That, instead of judging them and trying to dismiss them, I should notice these thoughts and then let them float out of my mind like clouds across a sky. It didn't always work, but it was a start.

Since then, I've discovered that, for me, meditation is the best way to help clear my mind of too many thoughts – although I'm glad to say that I've never had such dreadful intrusive thoughts again. However, I was only able to master meditation techniques once I was away from the drama and the strain of an abusive relationship and living on my own in the quiet seclusion of my second apartment.

My Dark Night of the Soul

Immediately after Consy's passing, I was devastated and grieving but, as I've explained, I wasn't aware of being depressed as such. With the angelic help of my mum and baby Consy, I'd found my purpose and I was gently working my way through my grief by sharing my experiences online with a growing number of women who were going through similar things in their own lives.

Obviously, I still had to face the challenges of removing myself from a damaging relationship with a narcissist, but I was getting there. Bizarrely, it was what would ultimately turn out to be my salvation that, at the time, proved to be my downfall.

As part of my spiritual quest (and in a bid to get away from Tom), I booked myself into a retreat in Bali in June 2019. It was blissful to be among like-minded people, to forget my troubles temporarily and to find some peace of mind. I totally immersed myself in the experience – it was balm to my soul.

However, when I returned to the UK and the stark reality of ordinary life, I felt overloaded and depressed. I'd changed and yet nothing around me had changed. I kept asking myself, *Why am I back in this apartment? Tom's still down the road, still doing the same stuff, while I'm trying to deal with the grief of losing our baby.* And the busy-ness of living in a town after the tranquillity of a tropical island was crushing me.

{ MALIN'S MANTRAS }

Only you can break out of the cycle of negative thinking. No one can do it for you. Sometimes we underestimate the power of our mind and how it creates the reality and circumstances around us. Remember that you have the power.

I couldn't understand what life was about any more. I didn't like it. I thought that living was painful. I wanted to be a soul. I wanted to become a spirit so I could join my mum and my baby.

I still had the Co-codamol tablets I'd been prescribed for the pain after my Caesarean section. I took all the tablets left in the bottle. I'd been looking for answers, but I didn't think that anything was going to save me. I no longer recognized myself, and I just didn't understand what the point of my life was. I didn't want to live.

After I took the tablets, I felt scared, but I just wanted the pain to stop, and to feel whole again. As I started to lose consciousness, I panicked and called the emergency services. As soon as the paramedics arrived, I conked out. They had to inject me full of fluids and medicine to reverse the effects of the overdose. They told me later that if they hadn't arrived when they did, I would have died for sure.

At the hospital, I was out of it completely. The medical staff were shaking me and asking me who they should call. I clearly remember that moment because I felt like I didn't have anyone to call. I started crying. I felt like such a sad fuck. I thought, *If I don't have anyone to call, what's the point?*

I just felt so lonely. The loneliness and all the other thoughts in my head were overwhelming, and all I could think was, *Why didn't it work?* It made me more pissed off that I couldn't even kill myself successfully.

In the event, the next day, my best friend came to pick me up. On the way home, an eagle flew past our car, and I was like, *Whoa, okay.* That was the sign I'd been looking for. After that, my spirituality kicked back in even stronger than ever. But not before I'd been through my very own dark night of the soul, which I very nearly didn't survive.

No Quick Fix

After my suicide attempt, I was prescribed antidepressants, but honestly, when I was on them, it was awful, and my head was messed up. I spent a week trying to get used to it, but I felt like a zombie. To me, the sensation of taking antidepressants was as if someone had taken away my soul, so I didn't feel anything.

Like everyone else, I wanted a quick fix to put an end to my mental pain, but I realized that, although it might take longer, the inner work and the healing had to be done. Taking the tablets just put that process and my life on hold. I needed to do the work and figure it out for myself. So, I took myself off the antidepressants, went cold turkey, and I've never been back on them.

Today, I'm happy to say that I'm glad to be alive. I now know I wouldn't attempt anything like that again. At the time, it was an accumulation of stuff, but the root cause of my misery was always Tom. He caused me so much suffering on top of all the other traumatic events that had happened in my life. He was the icing on the cake of suffering.

Thankfully, I don't give him a second thought any more, and my life has changed beyond all recognition. I've come so far since that fateful day.

OUR MENTAL WELLBEING

The vow I make to myself is always to look after my mental wellbeing. In the world we live in today, it's easy to get wrapped up in work or family life and find ourselves constantly trying to please other people. But we mustn't forget to give ourselves the same amount of attention.

Remember that healing is never linear. There will be setbacks and you must be gentle with yourself at those times. But, as I learned, you can go travelling, you can go on a retreat in Bali, but you've got to face your pain and your grief at some point. You can't just keep running away from stuff.

Yet, the main reason I know I won't ever try to commit suicide again is because I don't want to live another reincarnation on this Earth. Everything that's happened has happened for a reason. It wasn't my time to go, back in June 2019, or I wouldn't be here now. I believe that if you commit suicide, you have to come back for another lifetime because you haven't finished your soul contract for this lifetime – and I definitely don't want to come back here again. Forget that.

Reality TV and Mental Health

In fewer than three years, between June 2018 and February 2020, three of my friends from the reality TV show *Love Island* would be dead by their own hand, and I'd attempted suicide myself. That's a shocking statistic. Sophie Gradon, who was on the same series of the show as me, and a good friend, committed suicide in 2018, aged just 32. Less than a year after that tragedy, Mike Thalassitis committed suicide, only three months before my own failed attempt.

Their deaths hit me hard. When Sophie died, it changed my entire view of reality TV, television in general, and more. It confirmed to me that I was in the wrong kind of game and that, although I wanted to do TV, reality TV wasn't what I should be doing. I didn't need the crap that came with it. Honestly, I think about Sophie a lot – she was a very deep soul.

I felt that the show had failed in its duty of care to the stars it created. Sophie had complained to me that she hadn't got the support and the therapists that she'd needed. In my own case, I received a bunch of flowers and no phone call when Consy died, and I didn't hear from them at all when my mum died. The only times they've called were after Sophie's suicide and then again after Mike died. To be fair, after that second call, they paid for a therapist, but that was two months too late.

I know that some might say that the show can't take responsibility for looking after former contestants indefinitely. But surely they have a duty of care if the contestants are suffering and grieving in the public eye, as I was? It felt to me as if they took you in and chucked you out, and that they didn't really care about you.

I tweeted as much after Sophie's death and one of the producers called me. We had a good chat. I told him that I'd be happy to help future contestants as I'd been through it, and I explained about the importance of putting aftercare in place. His argument was that contestants are given a psychological questionnaire before they enter the villa and are asked if they've ever felt suicidal or self-harmed.

But are you really going to admit to being suicidal before going on the biggest reality show on TV? In truth, no one's going to pass up the chance of getting a new career from appearing on *Love Island*, so the questionnaire isn't worth the paper it's written on. I know the reasons behind every suicide are complex, but I really feel that reality TV culture and fast fame are partly to blame.

Sadly, it took the publicity surrounding the suicide of my friend Caroline Flack in February 2020 for things to start to change in the reality TV world. I believe that today, more stringent measures of care are being put in place. We'll see. I hope so. Caroline messaged me just two days before her death, saying, 'There's only so much I can take.' I was really worried about her and messaged her, but once you've reached that state of mind, I think it's hard for anyone without the right specialist training to help.

What I can say for sure is that I'm very lucky to have had the awakening that I had. If I hadn't found spirituality and my soul purpose after Consy died, I would have been among those reality TV star suicides, one hundred per cent. There would have been no reason to be alive otherwise.

The Final Hurdle

I had one last obstacle to overcome before I could develop my own routines for good mental health – the court case against Tom on assault charges. In the months leading up to that case in October 2020, there was a huge cloud hanging over my head, and while it was there, I couldn't be fully free and trust in my spiritual practices and meditation. And yet, little signs, such as the double figures on the clock or radio whenever the police called me with an update, helped me to trust in the process and have faith.

I hated feeling fettered in that way and unable to be the fully spiritual person I wanted to be. The anxiety around wanting to get justice was hard to bear, and I was worried that I wouldn't be believed. Worse still, I feared further attacks or reprisals by Tom, and I was afraid of every little sound at night in case someone was trying to break in. In part, this anxiety was a symptom of the PTSD I'd suffered since I'd been raped, but the fear was all too real.

Even though I knew in my heart that meditation and my other spiritual practices could help me to cope, I found it hard to stick to a spiritual routine. I actually bought a 'court case aromatherapy bath oil' which, looking back, makes me laugh because it sounds so ridiculous. But I bathed in it every bloody night! Apparently, it was blessed, and intentions were set into it. I don't know if it worked or not, but Tom changed his plea at the last minute, and I felt that there had been some angelic intervention which meant I never had to go to court.

Finding Freedom

Once I was free from Tom's aggression and oppression, I felt as if I'd thrown the shackles off my ankles. I knew I'd never go back to being bullied and beaten by anyone ever again.

In the same way, when I healed from anxiety and depression and I found self-love, I felt as though I'd freed my mind. I was free from concern; my thoughts were free; I was free from caring about what society thought of me; I was free from pain, free from everything. I'd let go.

Whenever I see birds flying, I'm always like, *I wish I was up there with them*. I've always looked up at the clouds, the sky, the trees – you see so much more of this world when you look up rather than down at your feet. I think I feel an affinity with those birds and their freedom.

Not caring what people *think* isn't the same as not caring. I'm hugely compassionate for others when they find themselves in difficult situations, but I don't care what others think of me – I'm free to be authentically me. When I'm outside my head and I don't let anything control or dictate to me, that's my definition of feeling freedom. And that's a fucking good place to be.

My Good Mental Health Practices

I believed I'd hit my wall when I lost my little girl, but after that first week of seeking oblivion, I somehow felt my mum guiding me. It was as though she wasn't going to let me go through a period of victimhood again, like I did after her passing. I could almost hear her voice saying 'No, no, no, no, no. Okay, you're going through heartache and pain, but hell no, Malin, you aren't going to do that shit again.'

So, after Consy's funeral, it was another week or so, two weeks max, and then I was like, boom. I was very focused on work, which saved me. Talking about my own traumas and championing the causes that are important to me has helped me massively.

At around the same time, I started a routine of self-care practices that I know help me to stay in a positive state of mind. I don't mean self-care in the sense of having a candlelit, scented bath and passively expecting that to cure my depression. To me, self-care is an active thing. It means putting effort into changing your habits, changing what you eat, changing how you feel. If you know what works for you, you can put measures in place when you see or feel signs that you're slipping back into a dark place.

It was hugely beneficial for me to realize that I could do things to help myself. I booked some therapy sessions because I know from the responses to my Instagram posts that talking about our problems and emotions is important. The charities that I'm an ambassador for do great work in this regard too – always reach out for help when you're feeling desperate, and talk to someone.

I also implemented other new habits to help myself. For example, I've learned that drinking too much alcohol is a downward spiral for me that leads to bad choices and low mood, so I limit myself to the odd glass or two of wine now and again. I drink to be sociable, not to get drunk.

I eat healthily, and that also makes a big difference to my mood. As I said earlier, I don't eat a lot of meat because it makes my digestion sluggish and I feel bloated after, but I eat a lot of fish and plenty of fresh fruit and vegetables. I'm a big fan of a morning smoothie with all that good, fresh stuff thrown in. Getting the right nutrients is definitely a mood enhancer.

How about doing some exercise to clear the mind? That's proper self-care for me. I know that if I get out in the fresh air for a walk or a run, or if I do a boxing session, I'll feel much better, even if I don't much feel like doing it beforehand. The feedback I get from my social media suggests that exercise is a good tool against depression for others, too.

> ⋆★ **Vibing High** ⋆★
>
> Whatever your mood, get up! Go and have a shower, do you hair, do your makeup – even if you're not going anywhere. Do some exercise. Eat good food. Make yourself feel good. Take action.

I've always used visualization for manifesting, but I also use it as part of my self-care routine. Just seeing myself as happy – on a beach or laughing with friends, perhaps, or my career going well. I envision it all and it helps my mood. In fact, Dr Joe Dispenza, an author and educator who I listen to a lot, says that the mind doesn't know the difference between *thinking* you're happy and *being* happy. So, you gotta keep seeing yourself in that happy state.

Now I know that will ring alarm bells for those who say that you can't act happy when you're depressed. And that's true, but all these self-care strategies combined can help all of us, and I believe that sending out the right energy was hugely important on my healing journey.

I've learned an awful lot on my path to good mental health. I understand what it's like for people who find themselves stuck in the grim tunnel vision of anxiety and depression, because I've been there. I'm so glad and grateful to say that I don't think I'll ever be depressed again. I know this because I'm now so awake and so aware of life itself. My pineal gland is buzzing. My view of the world has changed.

I look around me and I'm like, 'Yeah, this isn't real. This is energy.' People must think I'm crazy, but that's how I live my life. It's like the game of life, and it's fun. There's no turning back for me now.

Malin's Gratitudes

I'm feeling grateful for...

- Accepting my faults and being able to tap into my inner strength

- My self-care routine

- My determination

- The spiritual teachers I listen to and the books I can read

- My ability to keep giving

GROWING IN CONFIDENCE

Finding Self-Love

When I look back, I realize that I've always had an internal conflict tussling inside me. On the one hand, I was shy and lacking in confidence. When I was a youngster, it was due to my looks, but in my teens and early twenties, my self-confidence took another hit when I didn't get the result I'd hoped for in the Miss England competition, and when work dried up after I'd appeared on

Love Island. Self-love was at an all-time low for me; in fact, it was practically non-existent after the abusive relationship with Tom.

All that's one hundred per cent true. But here's the thing. On the other hand, I've always had a bit of drive inside to achieve something. There's always been this small flame of fight inside me. So, you can see how, over the years, I've felt conflicted. Scared to do stuff and put myself out there, but not wanting to miss an opportunity either.

I'm pleased to say that ultimately, I listened to the voice in my head that told me I deserved more, and self-love won out. But I'll be honest, it was touch and go at times. That small voice is what pushed me out of my comfort zone and into choices that anxiety and my lack of self-confidence didn't want me to make.

I really had to gear myself up to go on the stage for the pageants, as I was terrified. Even as cabin crew, standing in the aisle in front of all the passengers doing the safety procedure made me so nervous, but I made myself do it each time.

Even before I educated myself during my spiritual awakening, I instinctively knew that I had to actively take steps and measures towards self-love, and I had to overcome my shyness and lack of confidence if I was to achieve the goals that I'd set for myself.

The Dangers of Comparison

One of the biggest challenges to my self-confidence came after *Love Island,* when I started comparing myself to the other contestants, especially the girls. I kept asking myself, *Is it me? What's wrong with me? Am I not good enough? Don't I look good enough? Is there not enough about me?* That victim mentality was a major obstacle to finding self-love.

When you're looking at other people and watching what they're doing, and lacking belief in yourself, you only get further from who you should be. Of course, I didn't know it at the time, but that show was only supposed to give me a little bit of a platform; reality TV was never the right career for me.

When I was younger still, I lost my self-confidence after comparing myself to the popular girls at school or the models in magazines. I can clearly remember seeing a magazine in the waiting room at the doctors when I was in my teens and fervently wishing I looked like Kate Moss on its front cover. My body shape isn't like that, but it didn't stop me doing everything in my power to try and look like those models.

Constant comparison and searching for something that isn't in you, which is somebody else's path, simply gets you further away from your true self. I became more and more unaligned with who I am and my own character by trying to be something I'm not. For example, my character is getting up and having a big breakfast, eating and not exercising if I don't want to, you know. I'm not a natural size zero. When you start doing things that are uncomfortable for you, yet you persist anyway, that's when it becomes dangerous.

{ **MALIN'S MANTRAS** }

We give too many people the power to lower our vibration. Stay true to your own frequency.

Seeking validation from others about my looks by doing the pageants was the start of a downward spiral that only succeeded in contributing to all the insecurities I had already. It made them worse because it introduced the dieting and eating disorders, the need for hair extensions, the makeup, the add-ons... None of this was true to who I really am.

Narcissists Rob Your Confidence

By far the biggest blow to my self-belief and self-confidence came from being in a relationship with and living with a narcissist. The subtle way that Tom's behaviour ate away at me – so that I didn't realize it at the time – robbed me of my soul and my true self. He'd overload me with compliments and gifts, build me up, and then take it away from me again with cruel criticisms and by subtly undermining me. Bit by bit, he'd give out and take back until I didn't know where I stood any more.

Tom would attack my work so that I'd end up feeling worthless. He'd be like, 'Your work is a load of bollocks. It's embarrassing what you do.' Then the next day, he'd go, 'I've got a really good idea for what we can do on Instagram.' The contradiction in your mind takes you to a place where you start to doubt yourself and believe more in the narcissist's decisions. Narcissists are supreme manipulators, and I got to the point where I no longer trusted my own judgement.

If you've been caught out by a narcissist and you're beating yourself up for not spotting the signs sooner – don't. They're clever. If they'd said some of this stuff right from the start, you'd be like, 'Don't speak to me like that.' But they don't – it's all praise at the beginning and then they work slowly at undermining your confidence. They're experts at it.

In the end, it all boils down to control. They want you to be a certain way, to behave a certain way. They have you all wrapped up – that's to say, wrapped around their little finger. For me, the worst aspect was Tom's controlling behaviour, which made me feel inadequate, unworthy. I wondered why. It triggered all my childhood self-doubts about my appearance.

My friends kept reassuring me that he was lucky to have me, but I couldn't believe them. There was only one person I wanted validation from and that was Tom – the guy who took my heart and my soul. It's sad, but that's just how our brain works. We want endorsement from the person we think we love, and nobody else's opinion counts as much.

{ **MALIN'S MANTRAS** }

Please understand that a person can be obsessed with you and not even love you for real. Obsession isn't love. Infatuation isn't love. Love is love. It either is or it isn't. Recognize the difference.

Sadly, that's how narcissists control you; that's exactly how they want you to be. They keep you in your place by making you believe that their bad behaviour is your fault. It's all about stripping you of your identity. Slowly, slowly, but surely, they get you right where they want you. How messed up is that? After all he put me through, I learned some hard spiritual lessons, as I had to rediscover my true self and grow to love myself again.

Reinforcing the Lessons

Yet, just when we think that things have finished for us, the universe throws more stuff at us, just to confirm we've taken the lessons on board. So, despite being on high alert for narcissistic behaviour and rejecting a lot of potential boyfriends at the first red flag, 18 months after my last encounter with Tom, I let down my guard and allowed a guy to get close to me.

On our first public date, we were papped, and because that photo appeared in a newspaper, I found out that he had a separate life that he'd kept secret from me. It was the same cycle repeating all over again. The difference was that this time, my intuition had half prepared me, as I knew deep down inside that he was deceiving me. I didn't hesitate; I finished with him straight away and cut off all contact.

When I heard the truth, I wasn't heartbroken, more disappointed. And there wasn't an ounce of me that was truly hurt. I wasn't even sad, to tell you the truth. It was as if the angels had put a wall around my heart to protect me, saying, 'Don't worry, girl. It isn't going to affect you like last time.' It felt as though I was being tested. As if it was a karmic cycle and I had to show that I'd learned the lesson. The universe was underscoring the message for me, but this time there was no pain or suffering at all.

ENERGY PROTECTION RITUALS

I use a mix of different tools and techniques to protect my energy from negative people and harmful intent. Meditation is always my go-to technique, but my rituals include burning ethically sourced sage and spraying myself with Living Tree Orchard Essences' Defender from the Dark aura spray.

And the most powerful tool of all? Removing myself from any situation where I don't feel comfortable or which unaligns me. End of.

The Importance of Forgiveness

Since my awakening I've become a huge fan of the late spiritual teacher and author Ram Dass. According to him, 'we are all one'. That's why, when things aren't going right for our loved ones and those close to us, in part, our lives are unhappy too. When the whole world is going to shit, it makes us feel unsettled and unaligned. What happens to others affects us.

Essentially, you can't move on if you're holding on to anger and resentment. If you're begrudgingly saying 'I'm fine, I've moved on,' but you're still holding the pain inside you, your tormentor will still trigger you. True forgiveness is essential. I'm not telling you to run back to that person and say, 'I forgive you.' That's not it. Forgiveness is understanding and knowing that that person doesn't know any better – it has nothing to do with you.

Anger doesn't serve you. Anger weighs you down and prevents you from moving forwards. To be free of that person, to let them go and to be free yourself, you need to forgive them. Forgiveness is the key to unlocking your future and it prevents that person from continuing to have a hold over you. There are those who will insist, 'I can't forgive him for what he did.' But if you carry on living like that and holding that inside of you, it's not going to help you to move on.

The tool I used to help me forgive Tom after removing him from my life was envisioning myself giving him a hug and saying, 'I feel sorry for you that you're like this.' Empathizing and having compassion helped me. I'd say in my head, *You hurt me so much, but I understand that it's not me, it's you. This is your journey. This is your problem. One day, I hope you find peace in yourself.*

That's a very tough thing to do, don't get me wrong, but when you find yourself doing so, you heal yourself. You can't just go through the motions of saying the words without conviction, though. You must feel it – envision it. Meditate on it, even. A few times, I wrote Tom a letter. I expressed how I was feeling, all my emotions – I didn't hold anything back – and then I burned it. That felt really powerful.

So, I'd say to you, just put it out to the universe. Let the universe send you love and healing. Let the angels come through. Whichever way you want to do it – envisioning, meditating, letter writing – take the anger and resentment from within yourself and get it out, get it away from you.

❴ MALIN'S MANTRAS ❵

Self-forgiveness is essential for self-healing. As humans, we make mistakes sometimes. Carrying around the guilt of these mistakes prevents us from growing and reaching our full potential. For you to live your truth, you must forgive yourself and learn from your mistakes.

Finally, don't forget to forgive yourself for all that you didn't know at the time. Whatever crazy things I've done in the past, that was the choice I made at the time. That was where I was at. Why would I waste energy on thinking about how wrong I got it? Or living in resentment? Forgiving yourself is a major healing step. Do for yourself whatever you'd do for another person. It's vital.

Establishing Self-Care Measures

The depression I experienced while I was grieving for my mum and Consy, and when I was trying to leave Tom during 2019, was truly awful. I wouldn't wish it on anyone. Deep down, I knew I had to get myself out of the slump of despair and to take measures to protect myself from all kinds of negativity – whether that meant getting away from Tom, cutting false friends out of my life, or shielding myself from negative comments on social media.

For me, the first step was to take myself out of the equation and the abusive situation I found myself in by moving into a new place on my own and making some clear space around me. It's much easier to eliminate an abuser from your life when they're not able to see you and manipulate you all the time.

I recognize that this isn't possible for everyone, but if you can get away, even temporarily – get yourself out of the situation and gain some perspective – it can help so much. I went on two retreats in Bali that year to get away, to be in bliss, to get some healing and to try and make some sense of it all.

Rebuilding yourself after an abusive relationship and depression isn't easy. I needed to put some self-care measures in place. I have an inquisitive mind and I like to understand how things work, so for me, an important first step was to educate myself on certain things. So, plenty of books and lots of online research were the order of the day.

I was particularly fascinated by what makes a narcissist tick and my research, together with the Freedom Programme – a 12-week course for victims of domestic abuse (see the resources section) – helped me to understand how narcissists work and realize that the problem didn't lie with me. It's the smoke and mirrors used by the narcissist.

I applied the same curiosity to understanding what happens after death when my mum died, and the possible effects of the traumas I've been through. Ultimately, that research helped me to understand that all I will ever need is inside of me. I don't need confirmation or external validation from anywhere else.

I read a lot of books by enlightened leaders, too, such as Ram Dass and Dr Joe Dispenza; the latter's *Evolve Your Brain: The Science of Changing Your Mind* was a particular favourite. Every day, I'd listen to podcasts by Oprah and others, mainly Abraham Hicks. Even if it was only for 10 minutes, I built some education into my daily schedule.

Reading books and listening to podcasts helped me to understand that I needed to live through my heart, to see things from a different perspective – which is so hard to do – and to have compassion. I began to understand that Tom didn't know any better – he treated me that way because that was all he knew at that point in time. I started to feel sorry for him. This didn't happen overnight – don't get me wrong. It's really hard to do and it takes time, but that's certainly how I feel now.

I also went to a therapist – a lovely lady called Sian. She helped me a great deal with the after-effects of domestic abuse. It was hard for me to grasp how someone could do that to another person and she helped me to understand it.

In fact, I'll probably go back to her for some more counselling in future. And that's the thing with self-care – you can come back to whatever measures help you at any time during your healing journey, even when you feel like you're in a good place, just for a top-up.

People who know their stuff, such as the experts I listened to online and the authors I read, were very good for me. Vex King, who I reached out to, helped me a lot. He says that his latest book, *Healing is the New High*, was inspired by the questions I asked him while I was going through my relationship healing.

Vex understands the healing process so well and my questions about integrated healing and how to come out of trauma helped inform the topics in the book. Seeking out people who you aspire to be like and who you look up to really does help.

Protecting Ourselves

Self-protection is paramount in my self-care regime. Anything that makes me feel anxious or not good, I eliminate from my life.

I recommend you do the same. So, if you're in a relationship with someone who puts you down all the time, get away from them. If it's a friend who's not treating you well, stop seeing them.

Don't accept engagements or work that make you feel unhappy or unaligned. If there's an app or social media platform that's making you feel less of yourself, then delete the app, stop looking at the comments, and unfollow anyone who makes you feel less worthy than you are.

Recently, I was reading a newspaper article by a girl who'd been on my Battles podcast show. I scrolled down and clicked on the comments and there was one about me: 'Where's Malin? She hasn't spoken about her ex or her dead daughter in a while.' I instantly felt sick.

My first reaction was to wonder if that's what people really think about me. But then, what did I do? I decided to delete the newspaper's app because I found I kept scrolling and getting triggered. At some point, I'll go back on the app, but I go through regular phases of deleting it. If I know something isn't good for me, I put measures in place to protect myself.

★ VIBING HIGH ★

The ultimate in self-care is knowing your emotional triggers and not subjecting yourself to the energy that provokes them. Set yourself free of people who don't deserve you or your time.

You'll always know when you're out of alignment. Are things flowing effortlessly for you? You know, they should. If not, check around you. Who's around you? What's around you? What are you eating?

Are you exercising? Are you meditating? I know that life has its ups and downs, and we get redirections and stuff, but always look within when you feel unaligned and see if you can make simple changes to get back on track.

For me, routine is important in helping me stay on course. Implementing a regular self-care routine saved me. I knew I had to change something about my days, or I'd just stay in bed, unmotivated. Today, I look after my body and treat it as my temple. I make sure I eat well, that I get plenty of sleep and that I exercise or get out into the fresh air every day if possible.

And let's not forget the mind. My gentle morning routine after I wake up is journalling, counting my blessings in a gratitude practice, and lighting some incense or a diffuser. I meditate, put on calming music, or watch a motivational video on YouTube. I make sure my mornings aren't rushed and that I take my time. Then my whole day is set up. Try it!

Living with Self-Love

Without self-love, you'll continue to attract the wrong experiences and the wrong people into your life. You'll keep seeking external validation and never be satisfied.

But what is self-love? To me, it's believing that you need to treat yourself better. What does that mean? Well, it means understanding what you're worth. It clicked with me that to leave that toxic relationship I needed to truly *believe* that I deserved more. And with the benefit of hindsight, I realize that I wasn't capable of doing that for quite some time.

For a long while, I saw with tunnel vision, but I couldn't see any light at the end of the tunnel. All I saw was darkness. It's likely that if someone had told me that there was going to be light, that I was going to be free, and that I was going to be in a good place, I wouldn't have believed them. I think, in all honesty, you need to look outside that tunnel. You need to try everything in your power to understand that there's a bigger and better life waiting for you, and that you fucking deserve it.

Essentially, self-love must come from you. It's an ongoing journey with yourself, and nobody else. You can't get it from things, places, other people. It's something that you must search for yourself – you don't need anybody else to tell you that you're good enough. Self-love is a place of knowing, of self-discovery and self-knowledge, and you can't get that from anywhere or anyone else.

Nobody else has the keys to unlock that self-love, only you do. Sometimes, we lose the keys, and we need to find them again. But once you've unlocked that door and experienced that sense of freedom, there's no going back. It takes time, and many people give up on it, but the journey is so worth it. It's so liberating.

However, I want you to remember that you're only human. If you're still staying with a partner and you're in a dark place, if you don't understand your addiction to this person, or you don't understand why they're treating you in that way and you're lacking self-worth, don't put pressure on yourself to be healed or fixed immediately.

I think it's important to know that it's a journey, a process. Never in a million years did I think that I'd be sitting here writing about this now – how could I have understood that when I was back in the thick of it?

Put on Your Own Oxygen Mask First

We often spend so much of our days giving, caring, supporting, loving, working for, listening to, and showing up for others. Please don't forget to keep showing up for you; being there for yourself is the number one priority. You can't pour from an empty cup.

We need to understand that we can only see as far as our mind will let us see at that moment in time. You can hope for a different future, but you can't always see it. What I knew deep down was that self-love is loving yourself enough to no longer be treated like that; loving yourself enough to no longer put your body through starvation; loving yourself enough to have good people around you; loving yourself enough to look after your body and to meditate and look after your mind. I think I knew that even then, and that's why I took the first step to healing myself.

Through my journey, I came to understand that everything is temporary, so it's important to be in the present moment and to be at one. I try to appreciate the small things in life, the details, and to welcome change with love. I have a clarity of inner vision that I never had before – it's like looking at life through a clear lens. It's as if I've reclaimed my positivity superpower – and once you've taken back the power from whoever or whatever took it from you, you will not look back.

Looking for Life's Blessings

One of the benefits of living in the moment more is that I spend more time appreciating the little things in life and realizing how lucky I am. Today, I actively wake up and find things to make me happy. I look for purpose in life, and I needed to do that because I used to feel as if I didn't have anything. At times, I didn't even feel as if I had a reason for living, you know. Subtly, I changed my way of thinking from *I've lost my mum* to *Okay, my mum has died, but at least I have these people around me.*

I like to list five or 10 things that I'm grateful for – ideally daily, but sometimes it slips. I find that being grateful for what I have allows me to manifest and welcome even more great things into my life.

It's so easy to get caught up in a frenzy of always wanting more things. But stop, pause, take a breath, and look at what's around you and how blessed you are. Welcome all the blessings and abundance into your life because being grateful makes you feel good. Even if I don't always get a chance to write it down, I can be driving in my car, or watching the birds in my garden and I get that moment where I'm like, *Thank you so much.*

⟨ Malin's Mantras ⟩

Make today great. Get up and go. Start something new. Be who you've always wanted to be. Chase your dream. Get that one step closer to your goal. There's no point in giving up now.

The other day, while I was in the car on the way back from a very long photo shoot in Brighton, I thought, *I've got a driver, I've just done a cool shoot. Yeah, it took a bit longer than expected, but I'm coming back to a lovely home. My assistant Liv is going to be waiting for me. I've got Oprah, my dog. You know, things are fine. I'm blessed. I'm lucky.*

Being grateful can lift your mood just like that. It can take you out of victim mode and it can help you to take yourself out of a state of depression as well. If you wake up and you're not feeling great – your hormones are kicking in, life's a bit shit, and you're just feeling slumped – stop. Write down some gratitudes and watch how your emotions can change almost instantly. It works. Trust me.

Malin's Gratitudes

I'm feeling grateful for...

- My inquisitive mind. Never stop being curious, Malin

- Having the unconditional love of Oprah, my little dog

- Discovering true self-love and knowing my self-worth

- The abundance in my life

- Being able to forgive

Chapter 13

MOVING FORWARDS

Living Your Best Life

{ MALIN'S MANTRAS }

The goal is to find freedom. To be free of people's opinions, free from concern, free from fear, free from control and judgement. Find your Freedom.

Even if you can't see it, it's all working out for you. Walk with trust.

For a long time, I've wanted to share the story of the traumatic events and losses that have happened to me and shaped me – and now it's done. This is the final chapter of my book, but strangely, its ending marks the start of my new life. I feel like I've been through a rebirth, a rising from the ashes – which is why I've just had a tattoo of a phoenix inked onto my leg.

In many ways, I feel as though it's only in this past year that I've started to live, which makes me feel sad. So, let's not even call this the last chapter. Let's think of it as turning the page on the traumatic episodes of my previous life and embarking on the next phase, which I'm determined will be happier and more positive for the remainder of this lifetime.

Facing Up to My Past

While writing this book, I've had to revisit, scrutinize and reflect on my past life experiences, many of which have been painful for me to recall. You know that I like to keep it real for you, so I've tried to be honest throughout these pages about how it felt to go through the many traumas that litter my past.

As a result of this candid review of my story so far, I've become more aware of my journey and just how much has changed in my life – from my outlook and my beliefs to my lifestyle and my career. I've come a long way from the shy girl who hated her own body and appearance and who lost her way and ended up being battered but not beaten.

Whatever life's thrown at me, I've always been one for making the best of things and just getting on with it without fuss. Opening up about my experiences and emotions and delving deeper into my subconscious and into my hurt and my troubled past for this book has been therapeutic and strangely refreshing.

Nonetheless, reliving the pain has triggered me at times; I've needed space and time to re-centre myself after writing certain chapters, and there have been occasions when I've been like, *Shit, did all that really happen?*

If I'm honest, much of the past 29 years since my dad died hasn't been great – there's been a lot of pain, and dredging it up has reminded me of that. And yet overall, producing this book has been a rewarding and fulfilling undertaking for me – and I hope my story has been helpful and uplifting for you too.

My intention from the outset was that my story would offer some hope – even if it was to just one person about their own situation and future. Because what I can say with certainty is that I've finally found some peace, despite all that I've been through, and so can you. It's taken me a long time to get here and not every day is sweet – I can't sugar-coat it because that's not how it works.

It's an ongoing journey, especially with the healing. Some days I have a blip that can put me on a downward spiral, but now I'm much better at getting myself back from a dark place. I'm good at pulling myself out of it and preventing it from recurring.

I try to make the best of every situation, to look for the positives, and I see life very differently. So, I thank all the traumas I've gone through, because they've made me who I am today, and they've made me a wiser and more 'woke' person.

Although I am not my past or what I've been through, those experiences will always be a part of me: an add-on to my personality, if you like. I think there will always be a shadow of sadness about my soul because of those early traumas and losses.

Putting My Trust in the Universe

Facing up to my past head-on, instead of running away from it, has made me a stronger person, for sure, but more importantly, it has revealed my true self to me as someone worthy of love. Those traumas made me who I am today, and at long last, I'm confident and comfortable within myself.

As a result, I live each day as if it's my last, and I have a lot more gratitude in my heart for who I am. My work is amazing, and the friends around me are extraordinary — even though my circle becomes ever smaller because, as you now know, I'm very good at getting rid of negative people. I know that where I am is where I'm meant to be at this specific moment in time and I'm riding with it.

I'm flowing with the universe and putting all my trust in it. I enjoy living in peace and calm and I'm in a good place. I'm proud of my role as an ambassador for the stillbirth and neonatal charity Sands, as well as for the domestic violence charity Refuge, and I continue to fight for the causes that pain me. My activism has led to me being interviewed in the media and now I'm in the newspapers for all the right reasons.

⋆ VIBING HIGH ⋆

If your intentions are pure, everything that belongs to you will flow to you effortlessly. Keep a clean heart and mind for a great life. Keep vibing high.

I know that if my mum could see me now and all that I've achieved, she'd be so proud. She'd literally be like, 'Girl, you're on the right track. Don't let anybody take that away from you. I'm proud of you.' In all honesty, it's my mum who I most want to share my successes with, and even though I know she's watching over me, it's not the same as having her in her physical form.

That's the great sadness about losing your loved ones – they're not here at this very moment to share the experiences. When I find myself in a rut, I sometimes wonder, *Well, what's the point of me doing all of this? Who can I share it with? Who is it for?* And I need to remind myself that it's for *me*.

In summer 2021, while this book was already in production, there was a development in my life that means I now have someone else I can share my highs and lows with. A relationship has blossomed between me and a special guy who had been my friend for many years – we just hadn't seen each other romantically before. This new relationship is bringing me a ton of joy, and it's also resulted in us bringing another new life into the world – yes, we're having a baby together.

Our baby's due date pretty much coincided with the initial publication date of this book (we had to move the publication date to later in the year for that reason). Weird, huh? Even more spooky, the due date I've been given is exactly the same as the one I had for Consy.

Yet again, the universe is sending me signs. Naturally, this pregnancy is an anxious time for me after what happened with Consy, but I'm excited too, as having a family has always been my dream. It's just like I told you – this gift flowed to me when I least expected it, and the same can happen in your life.

A Changing World

I'm a firm believer that things happen in our lives for a reason and that we can grow and learn from the traumas that we experience, however hard and painful it may be at the time. It strikes me that the world has been through a trauma recently with the COVID-19 pandemic. It's been tough for so many people, but I'm seeing how, despite the tragic losses and personal cost, this pandemic has shaken everybody up, given us all cause for reassessment and made us look for a new meaning to life in a sense.

I think more and more people are open to and curious about spirituality. If I invite questions on my social media when I'm talking about spirituality, everyone wants to know more. Whether it's the Law of Attraction, manifesting, protection rituals or grounding exercises, people are a lot more interested and inquisitive now. I guess we're all realizing that there's more to this life than what we see right in front of us.

As the collective consciousness rises, people are waking up and their vibration is rising. You can just feel a difference in the people around you. You yourself have probably grown and evolved, too. If you find that you're feeling distant from some people who were previously important or just present in your life, don't be afraid to let them go. Trust that the right people will come into your life soon enough; the people that you need. You just have to have faith.

{ MALIN'S MANTRAS }

Trust the wait. Embrace the uncertainty.
Enjoy the beauty of becoming. When nothing
is certain, everything is possible.

Being awake in this world is a brilliant way to live because you feel so free, and when you then meet like-minded people and find your vibe tribe, life becomes really sweet. Nothing is ever a coincidence

— you can meet like-minded souls in the most unlikely places; I met a fascinating pair of woke souls in Dubai of all places, last time I was there. Just be open to new connections and change generally.

We all go through transitions in life, whether it's meeting new people, ending a toxic relationship, a change of work, or moving to a new area, yet most people don't find transition easy. It's too unsettling. I guess it's quite a rare quality, but I confess I'm not scared of change – perhaps because in my past, I faced so much of it. In fact, I've always loved change. I love being in new environments, with new people, and constantly evolving.

My view is that change equals growth. Without change, I feel like I'm not growing. In this recent rebirth, my circumstances have changed completely. I've taken on new and challenging work projects; I've changed my car; I've got a new dog to care for; I've replaced my phone because the old one was stolen; I have a new, shorter hairstyle and I've moved house twice. You might say that these are all material changes, which is true – but everything around me has changed, even so. Still, I reckon that the biggest transition for me in recent years has been in my spiritual beliefs and my outlook on life.

BEING SPIRITUAL

You can't say you're a 'spiritual person' and act/feel superior to others. You're not truly a 'spiritual person' if you look down on others who aren't as 'consciously advanced' or awakened as you are. Spirituality is supposed to make you do the exact opposite. It's about unity and equality. Whenever you feel like you're veering towards superiority, lessen your ego and check in with yourself.

Whenever I'm going through a transition and it's starting to feel overwhelming, I help the process by falling back on a good, solid routine. Before I moved into my current house, I lived in my PA's cabin for a few weeks while I was in transition. It was so cosy – a toilet, kitchen and living room with a sofa bed.

Even though I was living out of a suitcase and in a completely new environment, I kept my mind sane by making sure I stuck as closely as possible to my usual routine. So, every morning I meditated to keep me super grounded. I did my usual work schedule. I lit incense and candles around me. I stayed still and calm.

Whether you like it or not, change is going to happen at some point. It's inevitable. So, rather than getting anxious, angry or frustrated, embrace it. Transition is healthy, change is healthy. It represents major growth and major growth means a better version.

Spiritual Growth

Sadly, it took a great deal of trauma and heartache for me to start on my spiritual and healing journey. As I've told you, I was completely devastated when my mum died, but that's when I first started to get strange signs and weird phenomena going on, and my consciousness started to expand.

My mum's passing was the trigger that got me researching life after death, the repeating numbers that I kept seeing and other spiritual concepts. Back then, I thought I was completely broken and that my life couldn't get any worse. Unfortunately, the universe had other ideas, and I still had a lot more painful shit to go through before I was fully cracked open and ready to accept help and a different way of living.

After my awakening, my mindset around my past traumas just changed. I had an epiphany around the way I viewed myself and the way I viewed life. It sounds crazy, I know, but after I woke up, I just had a knowing about certain things, and I felt very differently about life in general. I found I could detach myself from a scenario, from the outcome.

Now, when things are going wrong or I'm getting frustrated and angry, I just detach myself from the situation and imagine myself as a floating soul. I detach myself from everything around me and float within myself. Then I can be at peace, at one, and the things that were worrying me or consuming me no longer matter.

That's not to say that I don't sometimes have an off day, or I don't occasionally find myself falling back into that downward spiral again. I'm only human after all. I can be really tough on myself when I slip out of my routine and drop the practices that I know help my life to run smoothly and keep me in a positive mindset.

What I – and all of us – need to remember is that life and healing are not linear. We all have setbacks. We all slip back into old habits occasionally before pulling ourselves up short and making progress again. It's only natural, and we must be kind to ourselves when that happens.

So, if you're wondering whether I consider myself the finished article, living my best life – absolutely not! I'm still learning and still growing, just like everyone else. It's an ongoing journey and sometimes I hit the inevitable bump in the road. When that happens, I try to give myself space and understanding. If I have a period of feeling low, of not wanting to meditate or not feeling like eating nutritiously, then I go with that for a while until I feel strong enough to get back to better practices.

Ultimately, I need to keep it all in perspective. Let's face it, I've had to overcome losing my dad as a baby, bullying at school and work, years of bulimia and a poor body image, being drugged and raped, losing my mum to cancer, an abusive relationship with a violent narcissist who landed me in hospital, and witnessing my beloved baby dying in front of my eyes.

When I look at it like that, it makes me realize just what a strong girl I must be, how I've turned my life around despite all these challenges, and that I should cut myself a bit of slack when I have a setback in my healing journey.

⭐ VIBING HIGH ⭐

Give yourself credit for everything you're accomplishing – both big and small.

Once you've lived with the comfort and ease of knowing that you're at one with who you are, and when you know in your heart that peace and happiness can only come from you and that nothing external can give you that, you never want to go back to your previous life of doubt and worry. Once you're awake, there really is no going back.

That's why I try to be present, mindful, in the moment and taking it all in, because I love the way it makes me feel – that's to say, calm and collected and not letting things bother me. I relish my new confidence and the self-love that I've discovered since going through my healing journey. My newfound clarity, inner knowing, and sense of peace are thanks to my awakening and my continued spiritual practices.

So, I continue to do my research, and to use my vision boards, gratitude practices and meditation. I also try to tap into my inner guidance system, asking for signs for certain things, while all the time looking for the positive in every situation. When things don't appear to be going my way, I remind myself that rejection is redirection – it's the motto I live by. And ultimately, I know that the universe and the angels have my back. What more can I ask for?

Looking for the Positives

Everything that's happened to me in life happened for a reason. I truly believe that without the trauma and loss, I wouldn't have grown into the person I am now. It's through my physical and emotional ordeal with Tom, and my grief and suffering after losing my mum and baby Consy, that I found my life's purpose. I certainly wouldn't be helping people in the way that I am now if it weren't for those experiences.

Even though it was devastating while I was going through those traumas, when I get someone on my Instagram telling me that I've helped them through some awful situation involving miscarriage or the loss of their baby, or that my experiences have inspired someone to leave an abusive partner, I feel grateful, proud and humble.

If you'd told me as an awkward teenager or during my troubled early twenties that, before I was 30, I'd be sharing my life story with you in this book and being a beacon of light, helping others through appearing in the media and on social media, I would never have believed it. It's crazy.

Some people may have let the kind of traumas I've experienced make them bitter and resentful, but for me, it's all a question of how you look at life, and I choose to look for the positives in every situation. Having been through a great deal and having lost sight of who I really was for a while, I'm now determined that I'll never settle for less than I deserve ever again.

For me, it took the trauma of being assaulted and losing my precious baby for me to take the necessary first steps to heal myself. I hope and pray that you don't have to go through the same trauma to start your own healing journey.

I hope you can benefit from my experiences. I can honestly say that the only way I could discover my self-worth and what I deserved was by being on my own and going through the healing process at my own pace.

I had to give myself time and a chance to think clearly, without anybody else disrupting my thoughts. Nobody manipulating me, nobody gaslighting me. By being alone and becoming comfortable with my solitude, I worked out that I don't need anyone else in my life. All the answers lie within me. And your answers lie within you.

A Bright Future

In this book and on my social media, I revisit my past to give you guys an insight into a particular time in my life and a glimpse of how I got through it, in the hope that some of it resonates with you and helps you to make changes in your own life.

One of the biggest lessons I've learned from all the traumas and the transformation that I've been through is that trust, hope and love are the most important things in life. That's why I just want to remind you all to be kind – to yourself and others. To spread love and positivity. To understand that we're all human – we all have our own journeys, and we don't know what challenges people are facing in their private lives. So, let's not be too quick to judge others. This world needs more love. We all need to open our hearts more.

You are more powerful than you know, and capable of changing anything in your life. Welcome and embrace healthy changes into your life and let go of old habits and practices that no longer serve you. Accept the necessary changes that need to take place in your life and let go of fear and worry.

Be positive about your future and every day you'll grow stronger and more beautiful. Every day you'll grow more compassionate, and your open heart will allow you to relate to others with peace, understanding, love and forgiveness. Your life is unfolding perfectly, and all in flawless Divine timing.

⭐ VIBING HIGH ⭐

Show the world the best you. You're here to be seen, in all your glory.

Like me, you'll become skilled at using every experience to grow. I've managed to find the positive in every situation, however awful it has appeared at the time. I've used my painful experiences as an opportunity to better understand myself and to see things from a different perspective, and that has changed my life forever. Through all the adversity and growth, I find myself in alignment, and once there, life flows more smoothly, and I see things more clearly.

Don't put any pressure on yourself to understand things instantly because you learn as you go. It can be a slow process – I'm still learning – but you have the time. Just take everything as it comes, be kind to yourself, and hold on to that positivity; it will stand you in good stead for every challenge you face in life.

Once you've finished reading this book, I'm hopeful and optimistic that you'll be better able to open up to hope – that you'll live your life free from concern, worry and pain and without fear of judgement by others. If this book helps just one person to find freedom from whatever hurt and emotional trauma they might be going through, I'll be happy.

Meanwhile, I'll be using all the tools and tricks of my new approach to life to achieve my own big ambitions for the future, which may well include working in the USA as a motivational speaker, expanding our family, and building a bigger platform to help other people. What I know for sure is that if those plans hit an obstacle, then it's for a good reason, and there will be a positive alternative outcome at the heart of it.

In the meantime, I'll continue to use my platform to shout loudly about the things I care about, to fight for the causes that pain me, to talk about the stuff that no one else wants to talk about, and to show off my beautiful, imperfect body for as long as it helps to change perceptions.

Manifestations for My Future

- I will live and work in the USA

- I will reach and help an even bigger audience of people who can benefit from me sharing my experiences

- I will have a loving family of my own

RESOURCES

Baby Loss
UK

» **Sands** (Stillbirth and Neonatal Death Society), working across the UK to support those affected by the death of a baby: www.sands.org.uk; helpline: 0808 164 3332; email: helpline@sands.org.uk

» **Bliss**, for babies born prematurely or sick: www.bliss.org.uk; email at hello@bliss.org.uk, or book a video call

» **The Miscarriage Association**: www.miscarriageassociation.org.uk

» **Tommy's**, committed to saving babies' lives: www.tommys.org

» **The Child Death Helpline**: www.childdeathhelpline.org.uk; freephone: 0800 282 986

USA

» **March of Dimes**, fighting premature birth: www.marchofdimes.org

» **International Stillbirth Alliance (ISA)**, working for the prevention of stillbirth and neonatal death: www.stillbirthalliance.org

» **Share**, pregnancy and infant loss support: www.nationalshare.org

Bullying
UK

» **National Bullying Helpline**, help and advice covering bullying in the workplace, bullying at school and online harassment:

www.nationalbullyinghelpline.co.uk; helpline: 0300 323 0169;
telephone: 0845 225 5787

» **The Diana Award, Anti-Bullying Campaign**, gives young people,
teachers and parents the skills and confidence to tackle all forms of
bullying: www.antibullyingpro.com

USA

» **STOMP Out Bullying**, anti-bullying and cyberbullying organization for
kids and teens: www.stompoutbullying.org

» **Stopbullying.gov**, information from government agencies on bullying
and cyberbullying, who's at risk and how to prevent and respond to it:
www.stopbullying.gov

Domestic Abuse and Intimate Partner Violence

UK

» **Refuge against domestic violence**: www.refuge.org.uk

» **National Domestic Abuse helpline**: www.nationaldahelpline.org.uk;
freephone 24-hour: 0808 2000 247

» **Women's Aid**: www.womensaid.org.uk; email: helpline@womensaid.
org.uk

» **The Freedom Programme**, a 12-week course designed for women as
victims of domestic violence: www.freedomprogramme.co.uk

USA

» **National Domestic Violence Hotline**: call free on 1-800-799-SAFE
(7233) or TTY 1-800-787-3224; or text START to 88788

Eating Disorders

UK

» **Beat**, beating eating disorders: www.beateatingdisorders.org.uk; email:
fyp@beateatingdisorders.org.uk; helpline: 0808 801 0677; youthline:
0808 801 0711

» **National Centre for Eating Disorders**: www.eating-disorders.org.uk; helpline: 0845 838 2040

» **ABC**, anorexia and bulimia care: www.anorexiabulimiacare.org.uk; helpline: 03000 11 12 13

» **Overeaters anonymous,** help for those struggling with compulsive overeating: www.oagb.org.uk

USA

» **Neda**, National Eating Disorders Association: www. nationaleatingdisorders.org; helpline: 1-800-931-2237

» **National Association of Anorexia Nervosa and Associated Disorders**: www.anad.org; helpline: 1-888-375-7767

» **Overeaters anonymous**: help for those struggling with compulsive overeating: www.oa.org

Sexual Assault and Rape

UK

» **Rape Crisis England and Wales**: www.rapecrisis.org.uk; helpline: 0808 802 9999

» **Rape Crisis Scotland**: www.rapecrisisscotland.org.uk; helpline: 0808 801 0302

» **Rape Crisis Northern Ireland**: www.rapecrisisni.org.uk; helpline: 0800 0246 991

» **Women's Aid**: www.womensaid.org.uk; email: helpline@womensaid. org.uk

» **Victim Support**: www.victimsupport.org.uk; 24/7 helpline: 0808 1689 111

USA

» **Rape, Abuse, and Incest National Network** (RAIIN): the nation's largest anti-sexual violence organization: www.rainn.org; National Sexual Assault helpline: call free on 1-800-656-HOPE (4673)

Suicide Prevention

UK

» **Samaritans**: www.samaritans.org; call freephone: 116 123; email: jo@ samaritans.org

» **Papyrus**, for people under the age of 35: www.papyrus-uk-org; helpline: 0800 068 4141

» **SOS Silence of Suicide**: www.sossilenceofsuicide.org; helpline: 0300 1020 505

USA

» **National Suicide Prevention Lifeline**: www.suicidepreventionlifeline. org; helpline: 1-800-273-8255

ACKNOWLEDGEMENTS

The Publisher would like to thank Xanthe Taylor-Wood from Touch Management for her support and help in bringing out this book. Claire Gillman did a wonderful job in helping Malin to tell her story, as did copyeditor Debra Wolter and proofreader Kim Bishop in their meticulous editing and checking of the text. And thank you, Malin, for sharing your wisdom with our readers. You are a shining star.

ABOUT THE AUTHOR

Malin Andersson is a mental health advocate, motivational speaker and body confidence activist. She rose to fame following her appearance on *Love Island* in 2016 and started her career as an influencer, but after experiencing life-changing trauma she decided to use her platform to promote healing, body positivity and self-love.

 @missmalinsara
@MissMalinSara

Listen. Learn. Transform.

Listen to the audio version of this book for FREE!

Gain access to endless wisdom, inspiration, and encouragement from world-renowned authors and teachers—guiding and uplifting you as you go about your day. With the *Hay House Unlimited* Audio app, you can learn and grow in a way that fits your lifestyle . . . and your daily schedule.

With your membership, you can:

- Let go of old patterns, step into your purpose, live a more balanced life, and feel excited again.

- Explore thousands of audiobooks, meditations, immersive learning programs, podcasts, and more.

- Access exclusive audios you won't find anywhere else.

- Experience completely unlimited listening. No credits. No limits. No kidding.

Try for FREE!

HAY HOUSE

Look within

Join the conversation about latest products,
events, exclusive offers and more.

 Hay House

 @HayHouseUK

 @hayhouseuk

We'd love to hear from you!